The Philippines Campaigns of World War II: The History of the Japanese Invasion in 1941-1942 and the Allied Liberation in 1944-1945

By Charles River Editors

Prisoners of war on the Bataan Death March

About Charles River Editors

Charles River Editors provides superior editing and original writing services across the digital publishing industry, with the expertise to create digital content for publishers across a vast range of subject matter. In addition to providing original digital content for third party publishers, we also republish civilization's greatest literary works, bringing them to new generations of readers via ebooks.

Sign up here to receive updates about free books as we publish them, and visit Our Kindle Author Page to browse today's free promotions and our most recently published Kindle titles.

Introduction

Japanese tank crew during the campaign

The 1941-42 Philippines Campaign

Those who had decoded and seen the Japanese communications in early December 1941 would not be surprised when they heard about an attack on December 7, 1941. They would, however, be astonished when they heard where that attack took place. Posted on the other side of the world, it was early on the morning of December 8 in the Philippines when American general Douglas MacArthur received news of the Japanese attack on Pearl Harbor hours earlier. With that, it could only be a matter of time before the Japanese attacked the Philippines.

Although MacArthur and Allied forces tried to hold out, they could only fight a delaying action, and the Japanese managed to subdue all resistance by the spring of 1942. However, in the aftermath of Japan's successful invasion, as the nation's military strategists began preparations for the next phase of military actions in the theater, their forces had to deal with a critical logistical problem they had not foreseen. The Japanese had to deal with large numbers of Filipino and American soldiers who had surrendered after a lengthy defense in the Bataan peninsula, but they were not prepared for so many prisoners of war because their own military philosophy emphasized rigid discipline and fighting until the end. They could not imagine a situation in which Japanese soldiers would willingly surrender, so they assumed that no other combatants would do so either.

On the night of March 12, 1942, MacArthur, his family and closest advisors were smuggled out of Corregidor on PT boats. From there they surged across the black ocean to Mindanao and were picked up by American B-17 bombers. They stealthily flew to northern Australia, a dangerous flight over Japanese-held territory, during which MacArthur casually remarked to General Sutherland, "It was close; but that's the way it is in war. You win or lose, live or die, and the difference is just an eyelash." At Adelaide on March 18, 1942 that MacArthur met the assembled press and told them, "I came through and I shall return." The words would go down in history, and MacArthur would eventually fulfill the vow.

The Philippines Campaigns chronicles the 1941-1942 campaign from the start to its notorious aftermath. Along with pictures of important people, places, and events, you will learn about the Battle of the Philippines like never before.

MacArthur walking ashore onto Leyte during the campaign

The 1944-45 Philippines Campaign

In the wake of the 1941-1942 campaign, Japan occupied the country and went on to expand their territory in the Pacific, while at the same time destroying the American presence in that region, but by the spring of 1943, American military planners had begun to create a plan to dislodge Japan from east and southeast Asia. To do so, parts of the Philippines were considered main strategic points in the potential Allied attack in the Pacific. The end goal of the Allied plan was an invasion of the Japanese home islands, in which heavy aerial bombardment would precede a ground assault. In order for this to occur, Allied forces would have to occupy areas surrounding Japan, with China adding to Luzon (the largest island in the Philippines) and Formosa (a large island off the coast of China) to create a triangle from which they could launch their bombers.

The Allied advance across the Pacific was based on this 1943 plan, with General MacArthur and his forces moving to the north through New Guinea, then Morotai Island, and then to Mindanao, which was the southernmost major island in the Philippines chain. At the same time, Admiral Chester Nimitz sent his fleet through the central Pacific, where they engaged Japanese forces at the Gilbert, Marshall, Marianas and Palau Islands en route to Mindanao. As the Allies advanced, American strategists became embroiled in a discussion over whether to stick to the 1943 plan, or whether to focus their efforts on seizing Formosa, from which they would be able to create a supply link to China and would also be able to cut Japanese communication lines to the south.

By the time the campaign started, Japan was on the defensive, but as they would prove in other places like Iwo Jima and Okinawa, Japanese soldiers would act fanatically before admitting defeat or surrendering. During this second major Philippines campaign, an estimated 330,000 Japanese died, and only a bit more than 10,000 were willing to be taken prisoner. In fact, some Japanese soldiers engaged in guerrilla warfare on the Philippines well after the campaign had ended and even after Japan had formally surrendered, prompting the Japanese emperor to personally make a visit and intervene to end the fighting.

The Philippines Campaigns chronicles the 1944-1945 campaign from the start to its aftermath. Along with pictures of important people, places, and events, you will learn about the campaign like never before.

The Philippines Campaign of 1941-1942

Chapter 1: Before the Campaign

The conflict between Japan and the United States had roots going back as far as the late 19th and early 20th centuries when America gained control of Hawaii and the Philippines and became a player in Asia and the Pacific at the same time that Japan was beginning to impose its power in the region. America's "Open Door" proclamation of 1900 also created strains in the relationship because it was announced in part as an attempt to curb Japanese aggression toward China. Further upsetting Japan was the treatment of its citizens in the state of California, where many social commentators spoke of the dangers of the "yellow peril." Following the San Francisco earthquake of 1906, city officials banished almost all residents of Japanese ancestry out of the city. Anti-Japanese sentiment in the early twentieth century was not only contained in California, as the entire West Coast as well as Hawaii enacted local policies against the Japanese, for instance, prohibiting them from owning property in some areas and regulating where they could live.

In fact, Theodore Roosevelt became so concerned about the deteriorating relationship between the two countries that in 1913, he sent an American fleet on an across-the-world goodwill mission that included a stop in Japan in an attempt to repair the relationship. Much of the tension between Japan and the United States stemmed from Japan's belief that it had reached the level of a world power. They expected to be treated as such, and they reacted negatively to all perceived slights against both the country and its citizens.

In terms of Japanese interests in Asia, the focus of their territorial expansion in the 1920s and 1930s was China. They invaded Manchuria but soon found themselves in a war of attrition in mainland China. In order to cut off supply routes that were aiding the Chinese, Japan occupied French Indochina, which drew condemnation from the United States. In response to Japanese aggression, America, in the fall of 1940, placed a steel embargo on Japan, stopped oil sales to them, and also increased aid to Nationalist Chinese forces. Following the lead of the United States, Britain also placed an embargo on Japan, who was threatening their colonial territories of Malaya and Singapore.

These constraints to natural resources increased Japan's hunger to expand. Not only were they trying to assert their position as a world power equal to that of European colonial nations and the United States, they also wanted to gain resource independence. By the late-1930s, their expansionary goals privileged gaining territories that would provide them resources that would allow the Japanese imperial machinery to run smoothly and efficiently and without outside interference. Japanese imperial plans were divided between two groups that held influence in the government: one that wanted to focus the country's expansionary goals north, toward Russia, and a second group which believed that Japan needed to look to the south, where the Philippines, Hong Kong, the Malay Peninsula, Thailand, Burma and the Dutch East Indies would all constitute part of the Japanese Empire's future.

This second group was able to gain predominance among Japanese leaders, and when their imperial endeavors began in earnest with an invasion of China in 1937, the Japanese military saw their eventual path as moving toward the south, where they could implement a plan they called *Dai Nippon*, or Greater Japan.

As with Europe, the United States initially played a cautious game vis-à-vis their stance toward Japan. After all, America was a democratic continental power secure in her own borders and with a strong tradition of isolationism. This attitude was strengthened by her historic hostility towards empire. Why should American lives be shed in a conflict which seemed to be yet another example of the old empires fighting it out for real estate?

Once the Germans invaded the Soviet Union, the Japanese no longer needed to worry about their border with Russia, allowing them to focus exclusively on expanding across the Far East and various islands in the Pacific. But by then the Japanese leadership faced a difficult strategic dilemma. Their ambition to build a large Asian empire could not be realized without the defeat of China, and the Chinese war had descended into a quagmire. A Japanese victory in China remained just about plausible, but in order to secure one Japan needed to maintain a large army on the continent almost indefinitely. In short, the war was draining vast quantities of resources and had become attritional.

Perhaps fatefully, Japan was of the opinion that an attack on British targets in the Pacific would inevitably bring war with America. From a modern perspective this appears a questionable analysis, given America's strong isolationist sentiments. For Japan in 1941 though, there was a chain of logic which ran from a need to secure resources to the identification of targets in the Pacific to the need to confront America.

At the same time, President Roosevelt faced a dilemma too. Though he had won a fairly easy election in 1940, the key issue during the presidential election of 1940 had been the expanding war. Both mainstream candidates adopted an isolationist stance, with FDR promising that American boys "are not going to be sent to any foreign war". It was clear that majority opinion across the nation took the understandable view that the country could and should stay out of World War II. Roosevelt however, had a more nuanced personal opinion. He saw that it was not tenable for the United States to operate in a world system dominated by dictatorships. Sooner or later, these irrational and violent regimes would threaten America as well. That was a hard-nosed strategic and political insight.

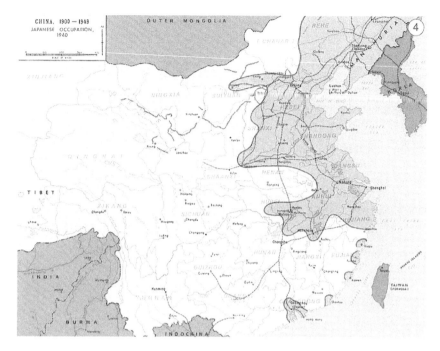

Areas of Korea and China occupied by Japan in 1940

If anything, it seems far more accurate to assert that both sides misunderstood the others' position and thus unwittingly took steps that would lead to the attack on Pearl Harbor. Far from covering up evidence of an imminent Japanese attack, Roosevelt and the military planned accordingly for a Japanese attack in 1941, and one of the most obvious targets for potential Japanese expansion was the Philippines, where MacArthur was bedeviled by a bunch of logistical and manpower issues.

While the U.S. went about expanding its navy, the military went about putting plans in place to confront Japan in the Pacific. Plan Orange specifically addressed a possible war with Japan and had been evolving since before World War I.[1] It envisaged a strategic withdrawal to San Diego, while the U.S. Navy could be built up and strengthened, followed by a progressive counter-offensive. This was conservative but also realistic. It assumed short-term Japanese superiority and accepted that the Hawaiian Islands and Philippines would have to hang on - and possibly face invasion - in the absence of the main battle fleet. These were not concessions that were easy

---

[1] And its successor "Rainbow 5" factoring in British participation, followed by the "Plan Dog" memorandum and Roosevelt's "Europe First" policy, during early 1942.

to make politically, and MacArthur would vocally make the case for a stronger, more proper defense of the Philippines.

While that step was not forthcoming, Roosevelt did have the main Pacific fleet sent to Pearl Harbor, where it was meant as a deterrent to let Japan know the U.S. meant business. At the same time, however, stationing the Pacific fleet at Pearl Harbor meant the U.S. was potentially leaving the Philippines exposed, and American military planners were constantly in fear of a Japanese attack there in late 1941.

As a result of these decisions, there was a marked asymmetry in both perceptions and capabilities as Japan and the U.S. stared each other down from across the Pacific in mid-1941. The U.S. was not ready for a Pacific war and did not want war at all, and though it was making preparations it was in no position politically or militarily to jump to the defense of the European empires in Asia. At the same time, the oil embargo indicated they were not going to underwrite Japan's aggression against China either. Without those resources, and operating under the potentially mistaken belief that aggression against Allied possessions would draw the U.S. into the war, Japan came to view the U.S. as the key obstacle to its ambitions. Both sides recognized that Japan had at least a temporary naval supremacy in 1941, and to Japan's High Command this gave them what they viewed as a small window during which to deliver a decisive blow that might secure a permanent advantage. The tectonic plates of war were shifting.

It is against this backdrop that the idea for a crippling surprise attack against the U.S. fleet in Pearl Harbor was resurrected, planned in detail, and delivered to impressive effect. The extent to which the results of the attack were directly attributable to Japanese planning and tactical prowess is, however, more open to debate, because the idea of attacking Pearl Harbor was actually an old plan dating back nearly 15 years.

The U.S. still had a chance to connect dots on December 6, the day before the attack on Pearl Harbor was launched. At noon on that day, the Army intercepted and translated a message sent from Tokyo to their ambassador in Washington instructing him to receive an impending 14 part message that was to be considered a counterproposal to American negotiations, and he was instructed to deliver the message to Secretary of State Hull at 1:00 p.m. EST on December 7.

That timing was meant to allow the Japanese to launch the surprise attack before the Americans received the message, but there was another clue that the Japanese were preparing for war. The communication also instructed the Japanese embassy to destroy its cryptographic equipment after receiving the 14 part message, meaning that they would no longer need to encrypt outgoing communications back. Such a step would only be taken if the Japanese had no intention of maintaining the embassy or using it for communications, which was a very clear sign that they were ready for war.

Although the United States and its armed forces had prepared for the possibility of an attack, they had not anticipated that it would be at Pearl Harbor, so far away from Japan in the middle of the Pacific. The attacks on December 7, 1941 took American forces completely by surprise, inflicting massive damage to the Pacific fleet and nearly 3,000 American casualties. Several battleships were sunk in the attack.

Chapter 2: MacArthur in the Philippines

General Douglas MacArthur's experience in the Philippines dated back to the 1920s, and he departed again for Manila in the summer of 1935 for a new challenge. Filipino leader Manuel Quezon wanted to employ a senior military advisor as the Philippines prepared for independence, and he trusted MacArthur, an old friend of his. Quezon was now the President of the Commonwealth of the Philippines, which was a transitional arrangement pending full independence. MacArthur's role was to design and build the new nation's armed forces.

MacArthur

The challenges facing MacArthur in his new job were daunting. He had to build armed forces from scratch on a shoestring budget, and the Philippines consists of thousands of islands with a coastline that is longer than America's. Internationally, Japan was now run by an aggressive military dictatorship and waging an atrocious war in China, and it also had bases on Kyushu and Formosa within easy striking distance of the main Philippine island of Luzon.

MacArthur's strategy was to build a small professional cadre able to draw on thousands of reservists in a time of crisis, similar to the American model he had devised years earlier. It would be organized into mini-divisions and supported by a tactical air force and small navy. For the latter, he successfully lobbied for the development and deployment of Patrol Torpedo (PT) boats.

MacArthur reckoned he had until mid-1942 to prepare for a potential Japanese attack, but he was beset with problems. There was inadequate support from America, and Quezon moved towards a policy of appeasement, lacking the political commitment needed for MacArthur's plan. On top of that, the Philippine troops had outdated equipment, there weren't enough of them, and linguistic problems precluded a homogenous force. Despite the difficulties, throughout this period MacArthur displayed an arrogance and optimism verging on the criminal. In several instances he deliberately misled the U.S. government on the Commonwealth's military readiness. In this, he was to be the architect of his own defeat.

Meanwhile, MacArthur's assistant, Dwight D. Eisenhower, could see where things were heading. The Philippines proved to be a trying place for Eisenhower, whose wife contracted an illness that nearly killed her there, and the cool Eisenhower clashed with the notoriously feisty MacArthur. Although Eisenhower claimed the falling out between the two was not as bad as has been suggested, his biographers have looked upon this time as a helpful experience that prepared Eisenhower to deal with the equally feisty British Prime Minister Winston Churchill and his initially disdainful commander Bernard Montgomery, who would at first openly question Eisenhower's abilities given his lack of combat service in World War I.

Disgruntled, Eisenhower found a posting back home, and MacArthur built a new team of officers to replace him. In mid-1937 MacArthur technically left the U.S. Army, but his relationship with his Philippine employers was at a low ebb too. It was not until July 1941, only five months before Japan's attack, that Roosevelt switched strategies and poured resources into the Philippine garrison. MacArthur was reappointed to the U.S. Army, promoted to Lieutenant General and given joint command of Commonwealth and U.S. forces. It would not be enough.

Eisenhower

Once Pearl Harbor had been attacked, it was apparent that the Philippines would also be targeted. In addition to the attack on Pearl Harbor, the Japanese attacked American possessions like the Midway Atoll, Wake, and Guam Islands. They also attacked the British colony of Hong Kong before invading the Malay Peninsula and taking Singapore. And finally, the government of Thailand surrendered to the Japanese without resisting thanks to pro-Japanese elements in the Thai government who convinced them of the futility of going to war with Japan.

Therefore, as Japan turned their attention to the Philippines, they had already had a number of successes in Asia, and their plans for enlarging the Japanese empire seemed to be progressing without problems. The invasion of the Philippines was to be carried out by General Masaharu Homma, who commanded a force of 43,000 men. Opposing this Japanese invasion force was MacArthur's forces, consisting of one division of 30,000 American soldiers along with 100,000 Filipino men, many of whom were reservists who had only received 8-10 weeks of training before the start of the conflict.

Homma

Prior to the beginning of World War II, American military planners had originally believed that the Philippines were not a defensible position against a potential Japanese invasion. Their initial war plans involved a limited defensive campaign that focused on protecting Manila Bay and denying the Japanese from using this vital port region. This plan was part of a larger American strategy against Japan called War Plan Orange (due to reasons of secrecy, Japan was designated nation Orange by American military commanders). In December 1941, as President Franklin Roosevelt began to favor a Europe-first strategy, War Plan Orange (WPO) was combined into a global strategy that the military command called RAINBOW (as it brought together the previous color plans designed for different regions of the world).

By 1941, the plan for the defense of the Philippines, which had been centered on holding out at Manila Bay for a period of six months and allowing an expeditionary force to dislodge the Japanese from the country, had been revised further. American military planners now believed that they could harass a Japanese invasion with a three-staged withdrawal to the Bataan Peninsula in a revised plan they designed WPO-3. The first stage involved a defense of landing positions, especially the beaches at Lingayen. Then, in the second phase, American and Filipino troops would begin an organized withdrawal to the Bataan peninsula. And finally, phase three involved American combat operations at Bataan, as well as several harbor islands such as Corregidor.

Nonetheless, the state of American and Philippine forces in the Philippines on the eve of the invasion was poor. The main body of troops came from the Philippine Army (PA), which was composed mainly of reservists, and their inexperience was compounded by the fact that the PA lacked modern weapons, equipment, and battle-tested officers. Even with the problems of the PA, MacArthur disagreed with American military planners and believed the Philippines could be defended, mainly by making up his troop strength through B-17 bombers and fighter planes. He believed that an increased aerial presence would allow him to better contest the beaches during the invasion, knock out artillery and mortar positions, and harass Japanese soldiers. MacArthur asked for and received clearance to obtain more aircraft to bolster his defenses, but these planes were not delivered in time to defend against the invasion.

As a result, the American army presence in the Philippines amounted to just 22,532 personnel in fighting condition on the eve of the invasion. Most of these troops were infantrymen, while another significant continent was made up of Philippine Scouts. The final piece of the American presence was the coastal defense artillery, which contained howitzers and mortars that could destroy enemy ships and also protect the vital waterways of the Manila and Subic Bays. American ground units were mixed with Philippine units, with the only exceptions being the 31st Infantry, which was composed entirely of American soldiers, and the 45th and 57th Infantry division, which, while made up of Filipino soldiers, had enlisted in the U.S. Army. The United States Navy's Asiatic Fleet, stationed at the Philippines, was under the command of Admiral Thomas C. Hart. These naval forces consisted of a handful of cruisers and World War I era destroyers, as well as a number of submarines. Like the ground troops in the Philippines, they were unprepared for combat operations in late 1941.

Hart

Unlike American forces in the Philippines, the Japanese had a strong presence in the region. The Japanese Southern Expeditionary Army, headquartered in French Indochina, was made up of four armies, as well as units that had gained valuable experience fighting in China and Manchuria. For the Japanese, the major problem they would face was not one of inadequate troop strength or experience but that they had to spread their forces out across the southern Pacific and could not concentrate just on the Philippines.

Chapter 3: Disaster in the Air

On the morning of December 7, 1941, the Japanese began their attack with the bombing of Pearl Harbor. Due to the time zone difference, American military commanders in the Philippines were asleep, but Admiral Hart was notified at 0230 hours on December 8th, Manila time. Due to the split command between the navy and army, General MacArthur was not notified at the same time, so the army found out about the attack half an hour later when members of the Army Signal Corps intercepted commercial radio broadcasts about the attack.

Even with this delay in information, both army and navy units in the Philippines should have been notified of the situation and begun defensive measures against the inevitable Japanese attack. Instead, because of problems relaying orders, there was a scramble to assemble the necessary soldiers, aircraft and submarines, and get them in place to contest the eventual invasion of the Philippines.

The Japanese invasion of Luzon involved two phases. First, from December 8-21, the Japanese engaged in aerial bombardment of strategic targets in the Philippines. One of the most important was the attack on Clark Field, which was the main airbase for American planes and its fleet of B-17s. When word of the potential invasion reached American and Filipino military commanders, army air corps officers took a long time to decide to attack nearby Japanese airfields to preempt bombing runs against the Philippines. They finally settled on attacking Formosa, which was the closest Japanese base to them. They believed an American counterattack at Formosa would stall Japanese air power and delay their ability to mount the invasion.

Adding to this delay was the fact that once their targets had been selected, the commanding officer at Clark Field, General Lewis Brereton, needed MacArthur's approval before he could launch his planes. However, in order to contact MacArthur, he first needed to go through Brigadier General Richard Sutherland, MacArthur's chief of staff. Sutherland was notorious for being very protective of MacArthur, and when Brereton contacted him for approval of the mission, Sutherland replied that MacArthur was too busy. He told Brereton to prepare his bombers, but that Sutherland would give final approval for the mission only once MacArthur agreed. Further delays due to weather pushed the timeframe for the Formosa mission back, and by sunrise on December 8th, Japanese planes were already in the air and making their way to the Philippines while American bombers and their fighter escorts remained grounded.

By 9:00 a.m. that morning, radar stations began picking up Japanese bombers heading toward Luzon, but as American planes were still being scrambled, Clark Field was attacked by two waves of Japanese aircraft, which were easily able to destroy the American flying fortresses and fighter planes that sat in lines as they awaited fueling and loading. A group of 21 planes from nearby Nichols Field managed to get airborne, but they were greatly outnumbered and easily shot down by Japanese pilots. MacArthur's Far Eastern Air Force lost most of its strength - nearly 100 planes, largely destroyed on the ground, in a matter of hours. In this short time frame Japan secured complete air superiority over the islands. Hesitation and bad luck had played their part, but the fact was that the defenders had not deployed sufficient fighters on Luzon. Unescorted B-17's were likely to have achieved precisely nothing against their supposed target, the Imperial Japanese Navy at Formosa. Crucially, the Americans were entirely unaware that Japan's superior A4M Zero fighter could operate out and back from Formosa without refueling.

Photo # SC-130991   Cavite Navy Yard burning after Japanese air raid, 10 December 1941

Pictures of Cavite Navy Yard on fire after Japanese air raids

Japanese forces were also able to score important naval victories in the Pacific against a number of countries. In an engagement off the coast of Malaya, Japanese forces destroyed the British battleships *Prince of Wales* and *Repulse*. American planes managed to sink the Japanese battleship *Haruna*, but Japanese attacks against the main American naval base at Cavite, as well as a secondary base at Olongapo in Subic Bay in the Philippines, destroyed their ability to resupply and support the Asiatic fleet, thus rendering the navy unable to play a significant role in attempting to repel the upcoming Japanese landings at Luzon.

Ultimately, Admiral Hart was subsequently ordered to move his fleet south, away from the Philippines, in order to avoid losing the main American naval presence remaining in the region. Thus, with the Japanese pressing a decisive advantage from the air, Hart evacuated most of his navy, except for the submarines, from the Philippines. The submarines were no match for Japan's navy, leaving MacArthur and his forces even more under siege. This decision enraged MacArthur, who exploded on Hart and asked him, "What in the world is the matter with your submarines?" MacArthur would later accuse Hart of cowardice to Secretary of War Henry Stimson, while Hart angrily shot back that MacArthur was " inclined to cut my throat and perhaps the Navy in general."

Chapter 4: The Japanese Landings

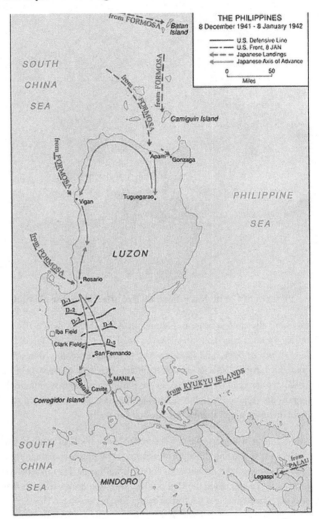

A map indicating the Japanese invasion points on Luzon

On December 10, General Homma ordered landings at Aparri and Vigan, thus beginning ground operations in the Philippines. The Aparri invasion was carried out by the Tanaka

Detachment of 2,000 soldiers, whose orders were to take Aparri and then seize its airfield, thus extending the range of Japanese aerial superiority. The Tanaka Detachment faced little opposition as it landed, created a beachhead, and then took control of the airfield.

A second Japanese landing at Vigan involved the Kanno Detachment, which again was composed of 2,000 soldiers. However, since the Americans were alerted to the landing at Aparri, the Vigan landing was attacked by some of the remaining B-17 bombers and P-40 fighters that had avoided destruction at Clark Field. American planes destroyed one minesweeper and two transport ships, forcing the Vigan attack force to pull back, but the next day, the Kanno Detachment again attempted to land. This time, they went ashore four miles to the south of their previous location, where they were able to gain a foothold and secure the town of Laoag and its airfield.

A third invasion force landed in southeastern Luzon, where 2,500 men secured the town of Legaspi and its railroad line by December 12. The Japanese then shifted their attention further south, where they launched an attack on the southern island of Mindanao with a force of 5,000 soldiers. The Japanese secured the airfield at Davao, which allowed their planes to reach as far as Borneo, as well as adding to their air superiority over southern Luzon. These initial attacks, which secured important airfields in and around Luzon, had the effect of isolating the island. Any attempts by the United States to reinforce their troops in the Philippines would be both dangerous and costly, making such an attempt from Hawaii or the West Coast of the United States extremely unlikely.

After this initial phase of the Japanese attack, American and Filipino ground forces prepared for the inevitable large-scale assault on their positions. MacArthur had at his disposal a force that on paper looked capable of opposing the Japanese land invasion, but it actually stood very little chance of holding out against the more experienced and better-equipped Japanese soldiers. Furthermore, while American pre-war plans called for the forces in the Philippines to resist until reinforcements arrived, the attack on Pearl Harbor and subsequent fears of Japanese attacks on the West Coast, which meant preparing coastal regions of Hawaii, Alaska, Washington, Oregon and California (as well as defending the Panama Canal), meant that aiding the Philippines was not a priority for military officials in the nation's capital.

Army artillery forces on the Philippines

Even with the Japanese taking up strong positions in the Pacific to utilize their air and naval power, Mac Arthur believed that a convoy headed by an aircraft carrier could break through and reach the Philippines. While MacArthur lobbied his superiors in Washington to attempt such a mission, military leaders understood that the Pacific Fleet could not risk testing that theory and losing a carrier. MacArthur also called for American allies to attack the Japanese, in hopes that the Chinese could begin a major offensive while the Soviets invaded Manchuria. This was not feasible, however, as the Europe-first strategy agreed upon by the Allies meant that the Americans, British and Soviets put the war in the Pacific on the backburner.

By December 22, the Japanese had switched tactics, moving from a focus on capturing air fields and aerial bombardment toward a major ground invasion. On the 22nd, 80 transport ships were sighted near the Lingayen Gulf on the west coast of the Philippines. The transports deposited the Japanese 48th Division, basically unopposed, at landing areas at Agoo, Caba, and Bauang. Helping the 48th Division, the Tanaka Detachment, which had earlier taken Aparri, moved south toward the landing area. The Japanese attack on Luzon through Lingayen targeted a drive toward Manila, which they hoped to quickly capture as part of their initial 50 day plan for conquering the Philippines.

A picture of Homma coming ashore at Lingayen

In most areas, Japanese landing forces were met by Filipino units. At Bauang, Filipino soldiers utilized .30 and .50 caliber machine guns to cause heavy casualties to some Japanese units. Elsewhere, however, a lack of artillery meant that Filipino soldiers could not mount an effective defense against the Japanese landings. Overall, the Japanese were able to effectively establish beachheads and then began driving inland at speeds that the American and Filipino forces were unprepared to oppose.

Military commanders believed that Lingayen would be a crucial site for a potential invasion because that location offered a direct route to Manila, the capital city. Due to its strategic importance, MacArthur had the 11th Division and Philippine Scouts' 26th Cavalry defend the Lingayen Gulf near San Fernando. He also sent the 71st Division to Lingayen from its original location at Mindanao. The 71st was tasked with stopped Japanese troops from moving south to link up with any invasion forces that landed at different locations on Luzon. North of San Fernando, Philippine Army units were positioned to contest two highways: Route 3 and Route 5. MacArthur also set two National Guard tank battalions in reserve to support the defense; due to his lack of tanks and armored cars, these units were in short supply and needed to be held back so that they could quickly move to invasion locations to shore up defenses.

MacArthur's main ground strategy did not depend on tanks or even American units. Instead,

MacArthur banked on his Philippine Army divisions to oppose the Japanese. He believed that members of the Philippine Army would be motivated by the fact that they were defending their homeland, and also that they would have an advantage in knowing the geography of the areas that they would be fighting in. However, thanks to the inexperience of the Philippine Army, their sheer numbers hid the fact that they would have a hard time standing up to the battle-tested veterans of the Japanese army, and as the Japanese moved inland, they quickly pushed the Filipino forces opposing them backwards. MacArthur became increasingly concerned that these units were being routed.

General Homma did in fact plan for his main invasion force to land at Lingayen. Homma committed the Japanese 48th Division, his best troops, to land at this location, where they would gain a foothold and then drive toward Manila for a quick end to the campaign. The invasion force that landed at Lingayen included 76 army and 9 navy transports, as well as additional naval vessels that had been diverted from the Malaya campaign against the British to protect the landing ships. With most of his fleet moving south, Admiral Hart sent six submarines to contest the landing party, but the submarines only managed to sink one transport vessel and a cargo ship. Unfortunately for Admiral Hart's Asiatic Fleet, many of the torpedoes that they were equipped with in the early part of the war had faulty detonators, so even when striking a target, they did not explode on impact.

Between December 22 and December 28, the Japanese landed over 43,000 men at Lingayen. In addition to the 48th Division, Homma landed additional units at Agoo, Caba, and Bauang, and they were all tasked with fighting their way toward Lingayen, where they would link up with the 48th Division. Like the Philippine Army units, the Americans also were unable to mount a serious defense, but they were able to offer some resistance with naval and air units. For example, an Australian-based B-17 force which was returning from a mission at Davao attacked a group of escort ships while a number of P-40s also attacked Japanese naval vessels. Both groups of planes, while contesting the seas, were unable to stop Japanese landing parties from coming ashore.

The speed with which the Japanese moved forced McArthur to commit additional forces to North Luzon in order to keep his troops there from being overrun. General Jonathan Wainwright sent units from the 11th Division, the 26th Cavalry, and Company C of the 192nd Tank Battalion to engage the enemy near Agoo. Even with the reinforcements, the American-Filipino forces continued to be forced backwards, and American tanks came under heavy fire from both Japanese tanks and bombers. The 26th Cavalry was one of the few units who did not retreat in the face of Japanese attacks as they held the town of Binalonan on December 24, which allowed retreating Philippine Army units to move south without being engaged by Japanese soldiers. When they finally abandoned the town, they had lost roughly 50% of their troop strength.

Wainwright and MacArthur

It was at this point that MacArthur decided to stop trying to protect the beaches and instead implement phase two of WPO-3, which called for an orderly retreat into the Bataan Peninsula. As part of the plan, American and Filipino forces created four defensive lines to provide a screen against the Japanese drive toward Manila. The resistance against the Japanese at these four defensive lines would give the defenders the time to implement the fifth and last defensive line, which would provide more heavy resistance. The engagement at the fifth line would then give the remaining American and Filipino units in the field the time to make their way to Bataan.

However, the swiftness of the Japanese invasion surprised not only military commanders, but also many Philippine leaders. As President Manuel Luis Quezon recalled, "Before noon of December 12, 1941, I received a telephone call from General MacArthur to inform me that he was sending his aide-de-camp, Lieutenant Colonel Huff, to see me on a very important and urgent matter. I told the General I would see his aide immediately. I was in my house situated on the cliffs overlooking the Mariquina River. When Colonel Huff arrived, he told me that General

MacArthur wanted me to be read on four hours' notice to go with him to [the American fortress at] Corregidor. I was shocked. I never imagined that I would ever have to take refuge on Corregidor."

Thus, Quezon and a few other important governmental officials were evacuated from Manila to the island of Corregidor on December 24, 1941. Prior to leaving, Quezon informed the remaining members of the government that in a joint decision with General MacArthur, they had decided to declare Manila an open city so as to save the city's residents from the aerial bombardment and land invasion that was sure to come from the Japanese. By declaring Manila an open city, Quezon and MacArthur hoped to save Manila's civilian population from the death and destruction of the invasion.

A picture of Japanese soldiers moving toward Manila

A picture of Manila on December 26

With the retreat of the American-Filipino forces toward Bataan, this meant that Manila would be left undefended. In implementing WPO-3, MacArthur understood that he would be unable to hold the capital city, but he also understood that attempting to defend it, which the Japanese believed would occur, would mean that his entire ground force could be destroyed in one engagement. At the same time, a siege and subsequent battle in Manila could mean the deaths of hundreds or thousands of civilians. Nonetheless, as a USAFFE communiqué reported, "Until Manila was declared an open city, the Japanese did not attempt to attack civilian installations from the air, but as soon as the army withdrew, including anti-aircraft protection, they immediately raided, hitting all types of civilian premises including bridges, convent, the cathedral, business houses and residences."

Even with these attacks, as the Japanese advance guard reached Manila, government officials tried to create a stable, peaceful environment by telling civilians that they would not be attacked unless they provoked the Japanese. As Jorge B. Vargas, who was appointed mayor of Manila upon the evacuation of Quezon, stated, "Manila is an open city. Let us be calm and proceed with our daily task and give the enemy no excuse to misunderstand our position." At the same time, the civilian government ordered all civilians to turn in their firearms and also disarmed the police force.

Japanese troops took advantage of the chaos that had accompanied their arrival to declare martial law, and they began to treat residents of the city in a hostile manner. Japanese soldiers acted aggressively toward civilians, often with little provocation. Looters were shot, while those accused of misdemeanor crimes were often tied to a post and forced to stand in a public location for long periods of time. Some civilians were attacked for little or no reason, and those who failed to bow to passing Japanese soldiers were subjected to being slapped in the face.

The Japanese military in Manila also engaged in widespread confiscation. Military officials took hotels, offices, and residential houses, and even schools such as the University of the Philippines were confiscated for Japanese military use. Japanese soldiers also confiscated cars and trucks from city residents, and they looted warehouses and stores for supplies like rice, sugar, and canned food. In essence, while MacArthur believed he was helping the residents of Manila avoid atrocities at the hands of the Japanese, they were in fact treated in a hostile manner as the Japanese occupied the city.

Chapter 5: Bataan

The 4ᵗʰ Marines in January 1942

Filipino scouts on horseback move past a tank in early 1942

For American and Filipino troops on Luzon, MacArthur decided that a withdrawal to the Bataan peninsula would give them the best chance at holding out while waiting for reinforcements to arrive from across the Pacific. The Bataan peninsula gave MacArthur a relatively defensible position in which he could reform his lines and conserve resources as best he could. Indeed, American and Philippine troops would eventually hold out at Bataan for five months before they were forced to surrender in the face of heavy Japanese attacks.

However, since MacArthur had originally planned on defending the beaches of Luzon and had rejected any idea of retreat, he had moved many of the supplies up to the front line. Now, as his forces were retreating, many were unable to bring the supplies back with them. For example, at Cabanatuan, American units positioned there were forced to leave 50 million bushels of rice, which was the equivalent of a five-year supply, and naturally, the loss of supplies in the retreat would have devastating consequences later on in the campaign. At the same time, military planners had based their strategy on a much smaller force than would end up arriving at the Bataan peninsula. Part of this was because extra air and naval units that were stranded on Luzon joined in the retreat, as well as civilians who joined the ranks of retreating soldiers while trying to get away from the Japanese invaders.

As the retreat was under way, General Wainwright was given the task of attempting one last stalling maneuver to provide extra time for the retreating soldiers. Between December 24 and

December 31, Wainwright and his PA divisions (the 11th, 21st, and 91st), along with the 26th Cavalry Regiment and the American Provisional Tank Group, stalled the advancing Japanese 48th Division by creating roadblocks and using the tank group's 75mm guns to inflict damage on the advancing Japanese infantry units.

For Homma and his Japanese strategists, prior to MacArthur's declaration of Manila as an open city, their single-minded goal was to drive to the capital and capture it, but when the Americans made the announcement on December 26th that they would not be defending the city, Homma realized that he would have to change his plans. The decisive battle over Manila that the Japanese had envisioned would not occur, and instead, he would need to defeat the American-Filipino forces at Bataan.

For the two retreating wings of the American-Philippine ground troops, the North and South Luzon Forces, the goal was to reach Bataan at the same time. If one group moved too quickly for the other, half of the ground forces on Luzon could be isolated by the Japanese and destroyed. Therefore, in early January 1942, the two groups moved in tandem as they made their way toward the end goal of Bataan. Japanese forces, after realizing that the final engagement would not occur at Manila, began following American and Filipino troops toward Bataan. The Japanese 48th Division, Homma's best, inflicted heavy damage against the 11th and 21st Divisions, who were ordered to hold the strategic point of Layac, and the ensuing engagements, involving tanks and artillery, inflicted heavy casualties on both sides. The 11th and 21st Divisions held their position under intense pressure from the Japanese, which allowed the straggling units from the North Luzon Force to find their way to Bataan. As this was occurring, the South Luzon Force also made its way to Bataan and also completed the crucial task of blowing up two bridges at the Pampanga River.

The Bataan peninsula had been chosen as the withdrawal point because of its natural barriers against attack. The area was only about 25 miles long and 15 miles wide, and in its center were mountains. The rest of the peninsula was mainly jungle, which provided cover for defenders. It only had two main roads running north and south, which meant that attackers would have trouble pushing into the interior of the region.

However, despite the natural protection that Bataan offered, the major problem that the American and Filipino troops there had was one of supplies. While low levels of food would mean that the soldiers would have to immediately go on half rations, they also lacked adequate supplies of weapons, ammunition and medicine. The original WPO-3 plan called for the soldiers at Bataan to hold out for six months before they could be reinforced for a push out against the Japanese, and even though many officers knew that reinforcements were not forthcoming, they continued to tell their troops that reinforcements were on their way in an attempt to keep morale up.

MacArthur split his American forces at Bataan into two groups. Wainwright commanded what was called I Philippine Corps, which involved 22,500 men stationed along the western portion of the peninsula. I Corps was made up of four divisions: the 1st, 31st, 71st, and 91st Divisions, along with the 26th Cavalry Regiment. Meanwhile, George Parker oversaw II Philippine Corps, consisting of 25,000 soldiers who were stationed along the eastern portion. II Corps was also made up of four divisions: the 11th, 21st, 41st, and 51st, along with the 57th Infantry Regiment.

Parker

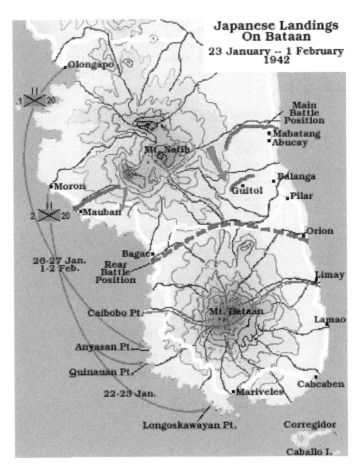

A map of Japanese landing points and American lines

There were three main defensive positions at Bataan. The I Corps and II Corps defended a main position between Mount Silanganan and Mount Natib. The I Corps was in charge of the region between the South China Sea and Mount Silanganan, which amounted to roughly four miles, and this position was called the Mauban Line. The II Corps then covered a region from Mount Natib's foothills to the shores of Manila Bay, which was called the Abucay Line. Mount Natib sat between the two, but because MacArthur believed the terrain of Natib was so formidable that nobody could cross it, he left a gap there between I Corps and II Corps. As it turned out, it would be in the gaps at Mount Natib that the Japanese would be able to make an attack on the American-Filipino positions.

MacArthur also created a second battle line, which ran from Bagac across the peninsula to Orion. This line was based on the WPO-3 plan and was supposed to be the last chance for the defenders to hold Bataan. Finally, an area on the coast near the Mariveles Mountains was a potential site for a Japanese amphibious landing, so MacArthur positioned the Philippine Constabulary, 4th Marines, and air force and naval personnel there. The overall strategy to defend Bataan involved using the terrain advantage to hold off the Japanese for as long as possible in the hopes that the war would eventually swing in America's favor and reinforcements would help them break out.

Japanese soldiers using flamethrowers against the Orion-Bagac line

For ground forces at Bataan, soldiers' diets were very poor. They were often given roughly 8 ounces of rice a day, along with a piece of fish or meat every few days. The usual meal consisted of thin rice porridge that was eaten twice a day. Due to the lack of food, many soldiers suffered from starvation and diseases associated with malnutrition. Along with the soldiers at Bataan were roughly 15,000 civilians, including government officials and ordinary Filipinos trying to get away from the Japanese invasion. The civilians were split into four camps in the interior of the Bataan peninsula, but the military had not planned on these extra mouths to feed, and the civilian presence further taxed their food supplies. American military commanders were also afraid that some civilians might be spying for the Japanese. They therefore posted sentries that restricted movements into and out of the civilian camps, and furthered the hardships that these civilians suffered.

For civilians, food was a major problem; most were not able to bring any food with them, so they counted on the army to provide them with their meals. Rationing for civilians was quite cruel, as they had to subsist on meager portions of rice, with one can of salmon also being given to every 20 persons per day. As one survivor of Bataan recalled, "Women and children would risk going as near as possible to the front to beg for food…During chow, one could see the most pitiable scene of famished women and children waiting at the bank of the river for soldiers to go there to wash their mess kits. Given a grain of rice left in the kit would be enough reason for from ten to twenty people to fight for its possession."

Another major problem for civilians was a lack of medicine. Along with the soldiers, civilians suffered from a variety of diseases such as malaria, dysentery, and malnutrition. Some unscrupulous physicians who were among the civilians sold the medicine that they acquired from the army for high fees. Military commanders eventually figured out that that this black market in medicine was developing and decided to stop giving medicine to the civilian population. Death was therefore a constant occurrence among the civilians: "There was a case of a family of a soldier composed of a mother and five children ranging from eight months to seven years. Somehow, the soldier, a sergeant, who was in the firing line, managed to get a pass to visit his family. Upon arrival in the camp, he saw only one member of his family alive – the eight-month-old child was being cared for by another family. The other members died of hunger and disease." (Buenafe, p. 100).

The Japanese made their initial foray into the Bataan peninsula by moving down the East Road with three infantry regiments: the 9th, 141st and 142nd, along with the 7th Tank Regiment. They tried to break through against the II Corps, and they also formed regimental combat teams which were tasked with supporting the main attacking troops and trying to push through gaps in the defensive lines that were opened up by artillery fire. As this was occurring, the 65th Brigade was ordered to move across the foothills of Mount Natib to the eastern coastal plain. Finally, the 122nd Regiment was ordered to move south along the west coast of Bataan, where they would have to cut their way through the dense jungle on that side of the peninsula. Once they reached Bagac, they would move eastward across the peninsula along the main east-west road at Bataan.

Along the foothills of Mount Natib, the Japanese 65th Brigade attacked the 51st Division near Abucay Hacienda. The 51st had been part of the South Luzon Force that had fought fiercely during the Japanese landings at Lamon Bay but had failed to stop the advance of the Japanese 16th Division. Ironically, the 51st was placed at the foothills of Natib because it was supposed to be a spot that would not see much action due to the presence of the mountain. This would supposedly allow the 51st a chance to rest after having been engaged in heavy fighting with the enemy for the past week. Nearby was the 41st Division, which held the center of that section of the line, and the 57th Infantry, a new regiment that would be fighting as a unit for the first time.

On January 9, the Japanese 65th Brigade began its attack on the Abucay Line when two Japanese regimental combat teams broke through defensive positions under heavy artillery fire. These advance Japanese units skirmished with Philippine Scouts, who were eventually able to force them out of the gaps that the Japanese artillery had created. As this was occurring, the

Japanese 122nd Infantry made its way west toward Olongapo, where they took a coastal defense position and then the town of Olongapo itself. On the night of January 11, the 65th Brigade went on a series of night attacks as they attempted to break through positions manned by Philippine Army units. The Filipino soldiers inflicted heavy casualties on the Japanese, and no territory was gained in the attacks.

The 65th also launched attacks against the center and western sections of the Abucay Line. In the center, Japanese soldiers pushed the 41st Division backward, but the defenders held the line and no penetration was made. Along the western section, the battle-weary 51st Division faced a series of assaults, and they were only able to hold on against them because reserve forces were committed to the area and helped the 51st to hold the line. Japanese artillery and air attacks against this section softened the defenses up, and eventually the Japanese found a gap between the 41st and 51st Divisions. On January 15, they began pushing the 51st Division back away from the Abucay Line. The Americans had already committed all their reserves earmarked for that area, and with no more ability to reinforce the section, they had to give way.

American commanders, understanding the danger that the II Corps position was in with the breaching of the western wing of the line, ordered a counterattack by the 51st Division with support from the 21st Division. This maneuver began to force the Japanese back in its early stages on the morning of the 16th, but when the Japanese 9th Regiment began an enveloping action to isolate the advancing soldiers, they stopped the momentum of the counterattack and opened a new breach in the line.

As this was occurring, the I Corps also faced attacks from advancing Japanese troops, but MacArthur had to focus his attention on the action surrounding II Corps, where a breakthrough was most at risk of occurring. MacArthur ordered the Philippine Division and the rest of the reserves to plug the gaps that had been created in the 51st Division. Meanwhile, Japanese troops under General Nara advanced as far as Abucay Hacienda, where they were met by the American 31st Infantry Regiment and the 45th Infantry Regiment. These two regiments tried to hold, but were overcome by the Japanese assault. The Japanese troops then continued their advance where they engaged more Philippine units. As this was occurring, Homma, believing that he possessed the advantage, made preparations for a large-scale assault on January 22nd that was designed to break through the Philippine Division and therefore the Abucay Line.

Japanese soldiers advancing in Bataan

MacArthur and his commanders understood that the Japanese were in a strong, central position from which they could move through the Mount Natib foothills and breach the defenses. Wainwright, however, was still convinced that Natib was too formidable an obstacle, and that the Japanese could not reach his I Corps from that location. Unfortunately, Japanese forces did in fact traverse the terrain of Mount Natib and Homma sent additional troops in the form of the 16th Division's 20th Infantry Regiment, along with artillery and antitank units and the Kimura Detachment that had been previously operating near Davao. Thus, as the Japanese planned their assault on the II Corps along the eastern section of the American-Philippine defenses, they also began an attack on the I Corps in the west.

On January 18, the Kimura Detachment began their attack against the 1st Regular Division at the Mauban Line. The Kimura soldiers were able to break through the Mauban Line, while other units moved in from the southwest and drove a wedge into the defense. By January 21, the Japanese had broken through the line and had isolated groups of American and Filipino soldiers, forcing them to retreat.

At the Abucay Line, the Japanese offensive of January 22 opened with heavy artillery fire to soften up the American and Filipino defenses, and Japanese bombers unloaded on artillery positions that attempted to fire back. After hours of fierce fighting, the American and Filipino troops stationed at Abucay Hacienda were finally dislodged from that location and forced to retreat. As MacArthur received reports about the intense pressure placed upon his soldiers and the new gaps that were opening up in the line, he decided to abandon their positions and withdraw into the interior.

The Japanese also planned an amphibious assault on the naval base at Mariveles, which would open up Corregidor to attack. Taking Mariveles would additionally block the communications and supply routes for the American-Filipino forces. To execute this plan, the 1st and 2nd Battalions of the Japanese 20th Infantry Regiment were tasked with landing at inlets near Mariveles and then fighting their way over cliffs overlooking the sea. As if that wasn't enough, units would have no reinforcements until the main force was able to overcome the American-Filipino defensive line.

The Japanese landing forces faced difficulties almost from the beginning. Choppy seas caused problems, as did American patrol boats, which sunk two of the landing craft. The Japanese also had problems with their maps, which were not detailed enough to provide navigational help, and their landing boats ended up four miles south of their target point. A second group landed even further away, a full seven miles from their destination.

Meanwhile, the defense forces at Mariveles were made up of airmen, marines, sailors, and Philippine Constabulary forces, but most of these men had very little infantry training. Naval lookouts observed a landing group of 300 Japanese soldiers and sent a portion of this mixed force out to attack them. The mixed force was unable to stop their advance, so MacArthur had to send regular infantry units to Mariveles to help out. Meanwhile, a group of 600 Japanese soldiers had been able to dig in at Quinauan Point, and another mixed force was sent to engage them. Again, these units were unable to dislodge the Japanese soldiers, even as more reinforcements were sent in, including tanks.

Finally, on January 29, the mixed forces, with reinforcements sent from the main line, defeated the smaller Japanese group of 300 soldiers, but at Quinauan Point, the mixed force had even more trouble against the Japanese. The tide only turned when the American-Filipino forces began using tank and infantry operations against the Japanese. With his invasion units under heavy duress, Homma finally ordered an amphibious rescue operation, but this too was unsuccessful, with only 34 soldiers surviving the attempt.

As the amphibious operation against Mariveles was ongoing, the Japanese continued their attacks against the defenses at the Bagac-Orion Line. Since the I and II Corps were in retreat, Japanese commanders tried to press their advantage through night attacks. At first they were unable to make a breakthrough, but on January 28, they were able to breach the line in two places defended by Philippine Army units. As the Japanese attempted to move through the gaps in the line, MacArthur ordered a counterattack, which stopped the Japanese advance but was unable to push forward. By early February, after days of heavy fighting, the Japanese realized that the Bagac-Orion line had reached a stalemate, so Homma withdrew his forces. Understanding that his men were fatigued and that he had suffered high casualty rates throughout his divisions in the Bataan Peninsula, Homma decided to wait for reinforcements to bolster his troop-strength before delivering the all-out assault that would end the campaign.

Chapter 6: The End of Bataan

All told, the Japanese army in Luzon had suffered 6,700 casualties, with more than 12,000 out of action due to sickness and disease. Homma asked Tokyo for reinforcements, but there would be delays in getting new troops to the Philippines in a timely manner. For example, the 4th Division had to be transferred from Shanghai to Bataan. Also, siege artillery based in Malaya and Hong Kong were sent as well, but it would take until early April for the bulk of these forces to reach Bataan, so there was a lull in fighting as the sides disengaged.

With the pause, some American commanders wanted to go on the offensive to retake the Mauban-Abucay line and push the Japanese further back. Although this plan was discussed, it was ultimately rejected, and in fact, the pause in fighting ended up hurting the American-Filipino forces because they were continually weakened by the lack of food and medicine.

Back in Washington, Roosevelt and his military planners by this point had concluded that the Philippines were basically lost, and they believed that keeping MacArthur, who had become a national hero, in the Philippines was extremely dangerous in case he was captured or killed. Roosevelt therefore ordered MacArthur to leave his command and travel to Australia. One of the reasons MacArthur had become so indispensable is that he had devoted much energy during the siege to his own self-promotion. A series of bombastic and often wildly inaccurate bulletins issued from his command were lapped up by the American press. Exacerbating the situation, MacArthur had accepted $500,000 from Quezon in back pay during the siege, which may also explain why MacArthur backed a proposal by Quezon to grant the Philippines immediate independence so that she could become a neutral state. Roosevelt rejected the proposal out of hand, and for MacArthur it was another example of playing politics, a dangerous habit.

Regardless, MacArthur, who had been commanding his forces from the stronghold at Corregidor, left the island on March 12th, with his family and several staff members. MacArthur made Wainwright the new commander and ordered him to continue to fight until he no longer had the ability to resist. Just before boarding the vessel that would take him away from the Philippines, MacArthur made a promise to his troops and to the people of the Philippines that he would return in the future.

MacArthur's arrival in Australia brought a new command, and America's highest award: the Medal of Honor. The inscription on the Medal read, "For conspicuous leadership in preparing the Philippine Islands to resist conquest, for gallantry and intrepidity above and beyond the call of duty in action against invading Japanese forces, and for the heroic conduct of defensive and offensive operations on the Bataan Peninsula. He mobilized, trained, and led an army which has received world acclaim for its gallant defense against a tremendous superiority of enemy forces in men and arms. His utter disregard of personal danger under heavy fire and aerial bombardment, his calm judgment in each crisis, inspired his troops, galvanized the spirit of resistance of the Filipino people, and confirmed the faith of the American people in their Armed Forces."

If anything, the medal was political because it was important to present the idea of a valiant defense and a heroic commander, and it certainly masked some of the poor decisions MacArthur had made during the campaign. But in fairness, MacArthur dedicated it to his troops, and besides, much stronger claims for the very same award could be made for his personal bravery both during World War I and at Vera Cruz. By winning the award, MacArthur and his father became the first father-son duo to both be awarded the Medal of Honor.

Meanwhile, the remaining soldiers at Bataan had the continued problems of lack of supplies, increasing casualties, and with MacArthur gone, the morale among the troops began to plummet. Additionally, by March 24, the first wave of Japanese reinforcements began to arrive. Japanese commanders placed their new artillery along the eastern part of Bataan and began shelling American-Filipino fortifications. The Japanese also began a new attack involving 11,000 men that took place near Mount Samat. Wainwright still had nearly 80,000 men at his disposal, but these men were mostly sick or wounded.

Japanese forces began their renewed attack against the Bagac-Orion Line on the morning of April 3 with a six-hour artillery barrage designed to soften up defensive positions. As one Filipino officer recalled, "The Japanese concentrated their artillery fire on an area about a kilometer wide by two kilometers deep…The Japanese big guns poured an unceasing stream of shell on that small area. A Filipino officer recalled having personally seen at least 17 flashes of fire – denoting at least 17 enemy batteries visible to the naked eye. " (Buenafe, p. 105). The area along the Bagac-Orion Line that had been hit "was so thoroughly and intensively shelled that, afterwards, it resembled no man's land, for the former green vegetation and trees of the jungle had been burned to crisp and only the charred stumps and trunks of trees remained in mute testimony to the severity of the barrage. It was said that out of the battalion of around 450 men and officers trapped in that area, only 150 were able to crawl out of their foxholes and dugouts to make a feeble attempt of resisting the advancing enemy." (Buenafe, p. 106).

After the barrage, Japanese then concentrated artillery and air attacks on the area near Mount Samat. Japanese troops were quickly able to move around the Philippine Army positions that had been targeted in the barrage and then began moving southward. These Japanese soldiers pushed the Philippine Army units back, and even with reinforcements sent into the area, they were unable to hold their original positions along the Bagac-Orion Line. As one American officer wrote, "[W]hen counter-attacks were ordered to relieve the dire situation there, they failed due to complete physical exhaustion of our troops." (Buenafe, p. 108).

Continued artillery and air attacks against II Corps forced them back further and further, and by April 8, American and Filipino troops began retreating to Cabcaben and Mariveles. Wainwright committed all his reserves to the fight at this point, and with no more troops to reinforce the crumbling defenses, Homma believed that he could strike the decisive blow with more one assault on their lines. Homma sent the 4th Division to attack Mariveles, and at the same time, the 16th Division would pursue the retreating troops, again toward Mariveles. As this was occurring, the 65th Brigade would move to the west to cut off I Corps from II Corps.

On April 9, the Japanese began their final assault, and American and Filipino soldiers were overwhelmed by concentrated artillery fire and fresh Japanese units thrown into the battle. The attackers reached Mariveles on that day, and American commanders understood that with II Corps in complete disarray and with all reinforcements having already been committed to the field, there was no way to stand up against the Japanese onslaught. Later that day, the American-Philippine forces on the Bataan peninsula surrendered to the Japanese.

Allied leaders discussing surrender terms at Bataan

Japanese soldiers celebrating victory after the Battle of Bataan

Even after the surrender came on April 9, the Allies intended to use Bataan as a rallying cry. That night, the Voice of Freedom broadcast struck a defiant tone:

> "Bataan has fallen. The Philippine-American troops on this war-ravaged and bloodstained peninsula have laid down their arms. With heads bloody but unbowed, they have yielded to the superior force and numbers of the enemy.
>
> The world will long remember the epic struggle that Filipino and American soldiers put up in the jungle fastness and along the rugged coast of Bataan. They have stood up uncomplaining under the constant and grueling fire of the enemy for

more than three months. Besieged on land and blockaded by sea, cut off from all sources of help in the Philippines and in America, the intrepid fighters have done all that human endurance could bear.

For what sustained them through all these months of incessant battle was a force that was more than merely physical. It was the force of an unconquerable faith—something in the heart and soul that physical hardship and adversity could not destroy! It was the thought of native land and all that it holds most dear, the thought of freedom and dignity and pride in these most priceless of all our human prerogatives.

The adversary, in the pride of his power and triumph, will credit our troops with nothing less than the courage and fortitude that his own troops have shown in battle. Our men have fought a brave and bitterly contested struggle. All the world will testify to the most superhuman endurance with which they stood up until the last in the face of overwhelming odds.

But the decision had to come. Men fighting under the banner of unshakable faith are made of something more than flesh, but they are not made of impervious steel. The flesh must yield at last, endurance melts away, and the end of the battle must come.

Bataan has fallen, but the spirit that made it stand—a beacon to all the liberty-loving peoples of the world—cannot fall!"

Allied soldiers listening to the broadcast

Chapter 7: The End of the Campaign

With the fall of Bataan, Japanese forces concentrated their efforts on Corregidor. There were over 11,000 American and Filipino troops on the island, and by including survivors who came to the island from Bataan, the number of troops stood at about 15,000. In order to take Corregidor, the Japanese would have to use an amphibious assault, and it took time to create a plan and move troops into place to execute it. Therefore, the assault did not begin until April 29. Prior to this, artillery and air bombardment targeted Corregidor's defenses, and these attacks knocked out many of the artillery positions that would have defended the coasts from invasion.

Corregidor was the best fortified of the islands in Manila Bay, which had relatively good defenses in case of invasion. This was in contrast to the preparations at Bataan, which were poor, and this lack of preparation played an important role in the problems American and Filipino troops had in defending positions there. In fact, in both 1933 and 1937, American commanders in the Philippines had suggested fortifying the Bataan peninsula, but instead the 500 square mile peninsula remained undeveloped in the years prior to the Japanese invasion.

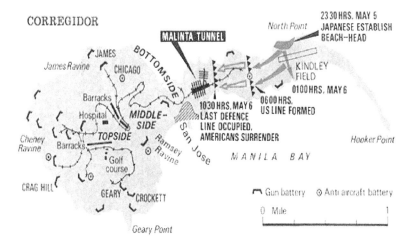

Map showing the Japanese landing points

The Japanese plan for Corregidor involved sending two landing parties of one regiment each. The first landing would take place on May 5 on the northern part of the island, while the second landing would occur on May 6 (this was because there were not enough boats to execute the landings simultaneously). Homma estimated that the invasion would take about a day before they captured the island.

The May 5 landing encountered problems, as American and Filipino troops saw the landing craft coming and fired their 75mm guns at the boats, inflicting heavy losses as well as destroying 31 boats. Even after sustaining such casualties during the landing, however, the Japanese troops who were able to make it on to Corregidor advanced and captured an artillery battery before coming upon a 500 man mixed unit of sailors, soldiers and Marines who tried to halt their progress. This mixed unit was unable to stop the advance of the Japanese landing party, who along with three tanks were too powerful for the Corregidor defense forces. By the afternoon of May 5, the Japanese had killed between 600 and 800 soldiers and had wounded another 1,000 men. Many of the men who made up the American and Filipino mixed forces were not trained as infantrymen, and although they tried to defend the beaches as best they could, they were overmatched by Japanese infantry units.

A mortar battery at Corregidor

The pressure the Japanese invasion placed on the soldiers at Corregidor, along with the fall of Bataan, had the effect of destroying morale. As the invasion of Corregidor continued, American and Filipino troops began to sense the coming defeat. As one officer wrote, "Wainwright might indeed boast to the world that Corregidor 'can and shall be held.' But the growing demoralization ate away the substance of the words. Only the hope of victory can made endurable the horrible sufferings of war, and in Corregidor there was no hope of victory. There was no future paradise to soften the rigors of the present; for Corregidor there was no future but defeat, no reality but the uncertain present." (Buenafe, p. 112).

At this point, Wainwright decided that he had no way of stopping the Japanese advance, and when they took the Malinta Tunnel, the main underground fortification shielding soldiers from artillery and air bombardment, he decided that it was time to surrender there. With the end of the Philippines operations nearing, Homma turned his attention to the southern Philippines, where he still had engagements ongoing at Mindanao and areas in the south of Luzon. In order to complete this last phase of the invasion, Homma once more had to request reinforcements. Military leaders sent units from the 18th Division, 5th Division, and 14th Army for this last portion of the campaign.

The first step was conquering the Visayan Islands, which sat between Luzon and Mindanao. MacArthur had originally placed five Philippine Army divisions at the Visayan Islands but had removed two divisions to help in the fighting on Luzon. The remaining forces lacked artillery, and the soldiers that made up the three divisions, like all Filipino soldiers, were quite raw and lacked proper equipment.

Philippine Army forces first saw Japanese movements at Visayan on April 9, when reports of a 4,800 man invasion force were sent to Philippine Army leaders. This invasion force was met by 6,500 Philippine Army soldiers, but they were unable to hold their positions, and the key city of Cebu fell the next day. They later lost a second key point at Cantabaco, and by April 12, Philippine Army forces had retreated into the north, where they organized a guerilla campaign against the Japanese that lasted for about a month.

On April 16, a Japanese force of 4,000 men was dispatched to take Panay. American and Filipino forces tried to slow the Japanese advance by destroying bridges and roads before engaging in guerilla warfare, but even with this resistance, the Japanese quickly took the island four days later.

The final phase of the campaign was the invasion of the island of Mindanao. Japanese forces launched two amphibious invasions of Mindanao, and by May 3rd, they had gained a foothold and had begun to move inland. The American commanders at Mindanao, seeing the speed with which Japanese soldiers were pushing inland, ordered a retreat into the interior of the island, which would give them more of a terrain advantage due to the mountains in that region. By May 9, the American-Filipino forces had been decisively defeated.

When American commanders at Bataan had surrendered their forces there, Homma believed the campaign was over, so he was angered when American and Filipino forces on Corregidor and the southern Philippines continued fighting. When Wainwright, on Corregidor, released command of Mindanao-Visayan to his subordinates there on May 6 and then attempted to surrender Corregidor, Homma would not accept Wainwright's surrender unless all American-

Filipino forces surrendered. Thus, Wainwright ordered all forces to surrender in a radio broadcast on May 7th.

This led to a conflict between Wainwright, MacArthur (who was now stationed in Australia), and the commander of Mindanao-Visayan, General William Sharp. MacArthur had ordered Sharp to ignore Wainwright's command and to continue fighting, arguing that Wainwright had become "temporarily unbalanced." Since Sharp was disobeying his orders, Wainwright was forced to remove Sharp as commander and then order his forces at Mindanao and Visayan to surrender. Some soldiers on Visayan disagreed with Wainwright's command and began a guerilla campaign against the Japanese. Other groups of soldiers around the Philippines also refused Wainwright's orders and escaped into the jungles, but by June 9, all organized resistance had ended.

Chapter 8: The Bataan Death March

The route of the Bataan Death March

Back at Bataan, when the joint American and Filipino force surrendered, they encountered various reactions by victorious Japanese soldiers. As the prisoners were being prepared for transport away from Bataan and into internment camps in the interior of Luzon, some Japanese soldiers began to take personal effects off of their new prisoners. As 2d. Lt. Kermit Lay recalled, "They pulled us into a rice paddy and began shaking us down. There were about 100 of us so it took time to get to all of us. Everyone had pulled their pockets wrong side out and laid all their things out in front. They were taking jewelry and doing a lot of slapping. I laid out my New Testament. In the Bible I had some pesos and a ten-yen note my first sergeant had given me. There was a captain in front of me and I whispered to him whether I should leave the Jap money out. He said, 'Well, I guess so. They said to lay everything out.' Something told me there was trouble, though. I don't know how it came to me, I guess the Good Lord was on my side, but when I could I reached down and picked up that ten-yen note, folded it up real small and tucked it in right behind my belt. After the shakedown, the Japs took an officer and two enlisted men behind a rice stack and shot them. We got to inquiring why they'd been shot. The men who had been next to them said they had Japanese souvenirs and money." (Knox, p. 116).

Japanese soldiers guarding POWs after the battle

Japanese mistreatment of American and Filipino prisoners was an outgrowth of the more general brutality of the Japanese military system. As Sgt. Ralph Levenberg recalled of an exchange between a Japanese soldier and a superior officer involving Levenberg's tinted glasses:

"I had a pair of specially made tinted rimless glasses. I got pulled out of the line by this Jap guard who wanted my glasses. When he pulled them off I tried to motion to him that he wouldn't be able to see much out of them, but he kept grunting and making it very clear that he was bound and determined to have a pair of American sunglasses. About then came along the tallest Jap I'd ever seen in my life. A lieutenant. He yelled, and this little guard froze at attention. The lieutenant came over and returned the glasses to me and indicated I should put them away. Then he turned on this private who was still at complete attention. The officer removed a small sword sheath from his belt and began beating this guard in the face with it, murmuring Japanese comments to him the whole time. That guard never wavered until he dropped completely unconscious. His face was just absolutely like he'd been run over with a tractor. I got back in line and kept my glasses in my pocket." (Knox, p. 116).

On the other hand, some American prisoners were initially treated relatively well by their Japanese captors. Capt. Loyd Mills of the 57th Infantry, Philippine Scouts remembered, "At one stop a Japanese sergeant, who spoke beautiful Oxford-type English, came up to me. He wasn't one of our guards, but happened to be around. 'You are going to find a lot of bad Japanese and you are going to find a lot of good ones. Please don't think that all the Japanese are alike as far as the treatment you are going to receive.' Then he opened up a can of sardines, and with some rice, gave them to me and the men around me. It was the first real food I'd had in days." (Knox, p. 117). As that account suggests, while the experience of the Bataan death march was generally one of extreme brutality and suffering at the hands of Japanese soldiers, not all of them participated in the mistreatment of American and Filipino prisoners of war.

The first groups marched out of the Bataan peninsula were fortunate to the extent that they did not face the same level of brutality as later groups, but even for individuals who did not necessarily face physical danger, rumors swirled about atrocities that the Japanese committed. Cpl. Wayne Lewis, for example, spoke of the psychological effects of Japanese treatment:

"The day after I surrendered they put me in a group and started us marching up the road. And I was on these damn crutches. They were too short. They were rubbing the hell out of my sides because they didn't come up to my armpits. Rumor had it that the Japs were checking the numbers in the group, and if at the next check point the numbers didn't match, they'd kill people to even the count. They we heard [a rumor that] for every guy missing at the next check point they were shooting ten guys.

By the time I got to Kilometer Post 147 I knew I wasn't going to make it. I started lagging behind. I couldn't keep up. What was scaring me was that I figured they were going to kill me. I was at the rear of the column by then, and a bolt in one of the lousy crutches began to get loose.

When we got near Hospital No.2, where I started from, I saw this guy wandering out of the jungle. He must have had malaria because he wasn't wounded. He was out of his head, but he had two good legs. So I told the sergeant who was staying with me to take this guy in my place. 'I'm going back to the hospital.' So I hit the jungle and managed to crawl back to Hospital No.2, where I stayed until Corregidor was whipped." (Knox, p. 125).

While the rumors may have been unfounded, there was no question that the marching prisoners quickly came to understand the dangers posed by some of the Japanese guards. Captain William Dyess wrote about the death march in 1943 and recalled the first murder he witnessed:

"The victim, an air force captain, was being searched by a three-star private. Standing by was a Jap commissioned officer, hand on sword hilt. These men were nothing like the toothy, bespectacled runts whose photographs are familiar to most newspaper readers. They were cruel of face, stalwart, and tall.

The private a little squirt, was going through the captain's pockets. All at once he stopped and sucked in his breath with .a hissing sound. He had found some Jap yen.

He held these out, ducking his head and sucking in his breath to attract notice. The big Jap looked at the money. Without a word he grabbed the captain by the shoulder and shoved him down to his knees. He pulled the sword out of the scabbard and raised it high over his head, holding it with both hands. The private skipped to one side.

Before we could grasp what was happening, the black-faced giant had swung his sword. I remember how the sun flashed on it. There was a swish and a kind of chopping thud, like a cleaver going through beef.

The captain's head seemed to jump off his shoulders. It hit the ground in front of him and went rolling crazily from side to side between the lines of prisoners.

The body fell forward. I have seen wounds, but never such a gush of blood as this. The heart continued to pump for a few seconds and at each beat there was another great spurt of blood. The white dust around our feet was turned into crimson mud. I saw the hands were opening and closing spasmodically. Then I looked away.

When I looked again the big Jap had put up his sword and was strolling off. The runt who had found the yen was putting them into his pocket. He helped himself to the captain's possessions.

This was the first murder. . ."

One of the main problems for prisoners being marched into the interior was a lack of water.

The Japanese for the most part did not allow prisoners to get water, so they could go long periods of time without being able to drink any. Capt. Mark Wohlfeld told of one incident in which American soldiers were finally allowed to drink out of a "buffalo wallow" during one stop: "Some of our young guys started asking the Japs whether they could have a drink of water. I looked to my right and saw a buffalo wallow about fifty yards off the road. It looked like green scum. The guards started to laugh and said, "O.K., O.K." So all these kids, eighteen- or nineteen-year-old enlisted men, ran for the water and began drowning each other trying to get a drink. The Japs thought it was hilarious. I noticed at the end of the scum some others drinking through handkerchiefs, thinking that would filter the bacteria out. Finally, a Japanese officer came along and began shouting at the men in the water. There must have been fifty of them, and they scattered and ran back for the road. That wasn't the end of it. This officer found some Jap soldiers who had been watching us and ordered them to pull out of the line any Americans who had water stains on their uniforms. When we marched out, after a short while we heard shooting behind us." (Knox, p. 128).

Sgt. Charles Cook also told of the issue of water. Due to the heat and humidity on Luzon, lack of water was a major problem not just physically but also psychologically as prisoners marched for hours on end with little or no water: "You didn't dare stop to get water. They'd bayonet you if you tried. I'll never forget or forgive them. Dag blast it, somebody gave orders to water their horses. Why not us? I know one time I broke ranks to fill my canteen with water. I heard this Jap holler. He was running up to me. So I ran through the back of the barrio, jumping fences and scattering chickens. I came back to the column and just mixed in with the men. The guard never found me." (Knox, p. 132).

Pvt. Leon Beck talked about the way the Japanese would use water to taunt prisoners: "They'd halt us at these big artesian wells. There'd be a four-inch pipe coming up out of the ground which was connected to a well, and the water would be flowing full force out of it. There were hundreds of these wells all over Bataan. They'd halt us intentionally in front of these wells so we could see the water and they wouldn't let us have any. Anyone who would make a break for the water would be shot or bayoneted. Then they were left there. Finally it got so bad further along the road that you never got away from the stench of death." (Knox, p. 134).

Since the march from Bataan to San Fernando took about five days, many prisoners inevitably began to straggle, and not surprisingly, the Japanese showed them little mercy. Captain Dyess noted:

> "The hours dragged by and, as we knew they must. The drop-outs began. It seemed that a great many of the prisoners reached the end of their endurance at about the same time. They went down by twos and threes. Usually, they made an effort to rise. I never can forget their groans and strangled breathing as they tried to get up. Some succeeded. Others lay lifelessly where they had fallen.

I observed that the Jap guards paid no attention to these. I wondered why. The explanation wasn't long in coming. There was a sharp crackle of pistol and rifle fire behind us.

Skulking along, a hundred yards behind our contingent, came a 'clean-up squad' of murdering Jap buzzards. Their helpless victims, sprawled darkly against the white, of the road, were easy targets.

As members of the murder squad stooped over each huddled form, there would be an orange flash in the darkness and a sharp report. The bodies were left where they lay, that other prisoners coming behind us might see them.

Our Japanese guards enjoyed the spectacle in silence for a time. Eventually, one of them who spoke English felt he should add a little spice to the entertainment.

'Sleepee?' he asked. 'You want sleep? Just lie down on road. You get good long sleep!'

On through the night we were followed by orange flashes and thudding sounds."

Picture of dead prisoners along the march

For those who weren't fortunate enough to escape but were still lucky enough to be alive, the march brought them to the town of San Fernando, where they were kept in pens in preparation for being loaded onto trains and taken to internment camps. However, the experience within these pens was not much better than it had been during the march. Prisoners continued to lack water and food and were exposed to the hot sun during the day. Many suffered from starvation and disease. Cpl. Hubert Gater's group was placed in a pen late one day and then removed early the next morning. Gater recalled:

> "Sometime after dark the Japs brought some cans of rice to the enclosure gate. A five-gallon can for each hundred men. These cans were not full. Who cared? Those close to the gate were fed. There was not enough to go around. There was no crowding or pushing. A friend helped a friend. Many didn't care. Besides being tired, many were in the last stage of malaria. Just to be left alone in the grass or dirt to rest, sleep, or die…
>
> It was a long night….Morning came. Malaria, dysentery, and complete exhaustion was taking over. We discovered many in the field were dead. Some perhaps the day before that we hadn't noticed. Men with dysentery lay in their own filth. The sound of men moaning and gasping came from every direction. As the sun came up, so did the odor and the flies.
>
> Later I talked to men at Camp O'Donnell who were behind us and arrived at San Fernando a day or two later. The dead had not been buried. The same terrible odor had doubled, and the sick and dying almost filled the area." (Knox, p. 148).

When the trains arrived to take prisoners away from San Fernando, they were loaded into hot boxcars with roughly 100 men in each. As Hubert Gater described of his experience on the train-ride, "We jammed in – standing room only. Into the oven we went and, protest be damned, the doors were closed. The three hours that followed are almost indescribable. Men fainting with no place to fall. Those with dysentery had no control of themselves. As the car swayed, the urine, the sweat, and the vomit rolled three inches deep back and forth around and in our shoes. Very little complaining." (Knox, p. 151).

While Gater mentioned men in his boxcar passing out from lack of air, Pfc. Jack Brady described prisoners who actually died while on the train ride: "It seems to me that once in a while our train would stop, and the Jap guards would open the doors so we could get some fresh air. Then is when we'd get the dead ones out. If we could, we'd lift the corpses and pass them over to the door." (Knox, p. 151).

After taking the train, the prisoners arrived at Camp O'Donnell, which the Japanese would use as an internment camp for American and Filipino prisoners of war. Camp O'Donnell was a partially completed American airfield located near the town of Capas, but the barracks at the camp were turned into a makeshift hospital, and the only supplies on hand for the prisoners were those that American and Filipino soldiers had carried with them on the march out of Bataan.

Unfortunately, the prisoners of war at Camp O'Donnell would not be covered by the 1929 agreement on treatment of prisoners of war that had been convened at Geneva, Switzerland. This agreement defined the term "prisoners of war" and also demanded that they would be humanely treated. Japan, however, had failed to ratify the agreement, in part because the Japanese representative to the conference, Isaburo Yoshida, asserted "that real improvement in the condition of prisoners depends, in the final analysis, on the humanitarian sentiments and good will of the belligerents." (Knox, p.154).

Furthermore, Japanese military personnel believed anyone who surrendered was a traitor to their country and deserved harsh treatment. In the Japanese military mindset, there was no room for surrender, but if one failed to fight to the death, they could commit suicide as an alternative. The concept that no soldier should be taken prisoner helps explain treatment of Filipino and American prisoners at the hands of the Japanese in the Philippines.

Life at Camp O'Donnell was harsh, and many men there suffered from disease and other maladies. For those who could still function, there were a number of tasks that needed to be done on a daily basis. As Pfc. Jack Brady recalled:

> "Unfortunately, there was no such thing as being laid up for a while at O'Donnell. There were people in much worse shape than I. Water had to be hauled, people had to be buried, wood needed to be brought in – all kinds of things needed doing. So in O'Donnell, if you could move, you did something.
>
> The place was organized very simply. You picked where you wanted to lie down and that became yours. Officers or senior noncoms selected the men for work details. Those men selected, of course, weren't that many. Most of the men couldn't, or didn't, move. The first detail I went on was where I loaded wood onto trucks and carts for use in the camp. We needed wood to make the fire to boil the water to cook the rice in.
>
> We had to have a water detail too, because the only source in the camp of reasonably good water came from one pipe. The rest of the water had to come from the river. If it wasn't boiled before it was used, it would kill you. It would take a while, but you'd die. The stuff had more germs in it than it had water. We carried the water to the camp in fifty-gallon drums. It took eight men to carry each drum – four men carried and four men rested. Because there was a constant need for water, this was a day-long detail. As soon as you made one trip, you'd go back for

another." (Knox, p. 161).

Not surprisingly, things weren't much better in terms of food. Prisoner Gustavo Ingles explained, "Well, our ration [was] given on the cover of the meat can, so if you put rice there and then you use a piece of wood to keep it flat, that was our ration.... So, you can find worms together with the boiled rice. At first we were throwing that away until one of the American prisoners found out that we were throwing it away. He said, 'Give it to us because we need it.' At first we didn't mind, and he told us that, 'We can't understand it, why you're throwing it away, that is protein.' So, I told him, 'Now that we know, we won't give it to you any more...' It was no more about the chemistry, about what to eat, which we didn't understand by that time. What we understand is only what entered the mouth, that's it's purely rice. Sometimes they put salt so that it would taste different."

As bad as conditions were for American prisoners, it was worse for the Filipinos. Their death rates were much higher than those for the Americans, and on top of that, they received even more brutal treatment than that given to the Americans. Sgt. Knox remembered the large numbers of Filipino dead: "The Filipinos were dying like flies. Carried in a tent-half buttoned up to form a tube, their bodies went by in an endless column. It never ended. Day and night the bodies were carried to the cemetery. I was kind of stunned by the death rate." (Knox, p. 164).

Death was a constant at Camp O'Donnell, and while some men succumbed to disease and other ailments, others just gave up. As the stories show, survival was as much about mental toughness and a will to live as it was about overcoming injury and disease. Those who failed to take things one day at a time instead looked at the long-term implications of imprisonment often lost the will to survive. This was a situation that Pfc. Wilburn Snyder spoke of in one of his interviews: "Not everyone that died died because they gave up, but many did. I spent much of my time trying to get two of my buddies to eat. That was the big problem. Many just said, 'Well, phooey, what's the use?'" (Knox, p. 167). Cpl. Gater spoke of a similar situation: " The theory of self-survival would bother me many times. Not only for myself, but for others. Can a man will himself to die in a two or three-week period? Mahatma Gandhi could go on a thirty-day hunger strike and survive. Some of our men seemed able to give up and die in three weeks or less." (Knox, p. 168).

One of the best ways to ensure survival was to make friends or get into a group in which the members could aid each other and pool their resources. Resource pooling involved a number of activities that provided larger opportunities for trading goods and services by creating networks with other individuals and groups and caring for members during periods of illness or injury. As Capt. Lloyd Mills discussed, "You tried to keep alive. Luckily for me I got into a group. That was the only way to survive. Generally, groups were made up of guys out of the same outfit. We tried to help each other. Someone would steal or swap for quinine. When one of us would get a malaria attack, the other guy would help out. I had a friend. We'd come over on the same boat.

He was out of the 31st Infantry. One night he came down to my area shouting for me. He said, 'You've got to get me over to the hospital.' He was really hurting; he had an internal obstruction. I told him, 'No, don't go over there.' He said that if I didn't do something for him, he'd die right there. I took him over to the hospital and found the doctor. Before I left he gave me his billfold to keep for him. They operated. He never came back. Anyway, back in his billfold there was a 100-peso bill. With it I was able to buy some stuff which I spread around in my group." (Knox, p. 207).

By the end of April 1942, about 9,300 Americans and 48,000 Filipinos had arrived at Camp O'Donnell. During the march from Bataan to the arrival at Camp O'Donnell, historians estimate the number of deaths were between 5,000-10,000 Filipinos and 600-700 Americans.

Chapter 9: The Aftermath of the Campaign

The Philippines campaign gave Washington important experience in confronting the Japanese. Pre-war strategies for the Pacific theater did not accurately reflect the resources or capabilities of American forces in the region. The American-Philippine force had delayed the invasion by turning a planned 50 day campaign by the Japanese into a 6 month battle, but military leaders in Washington believed that even had the Philippine Army been properly trained and equipped, their isolation relative to the placement of the rest of the American forces around the world meant that they would have eventually capitulated to the Japanese invasion.

The Philippines pre-war plan, WPO-3, was flawed, as the idea that ground forces in the Philippines would hold on until reinforcements from across the Pacific arrived were obsolete the moment the Japanese attack on Pearl Harbor began. The physical damage to the Pacific Fleet that the Japanese attack caused, along with the psychological effects of Japan's capabilities of attacking Hawaii (and perhaps even the West Coast), meant that reinforcing the Philippines was not possible. Additionally, MacArthur began his defense by rejecting WPO-3, instead moving vital supplies and manpower in an all-out push to contest Japanese landing points. Without an overall strategy, the Philippines defense suffered. At the same time, the army and navy had different aims and did not communicate properly with one another. Admiral Hart had orders to move his fleet south in order to protect it from Japanese naval and air units, but this had the effect of damaging MacArthur's prospects of contesting the Philippines' beaches where he would only have ground forces and no significant naval presence to help.

The loss of aircraft in the pre-invasion Japanese bombings of Luzon was also a huge blow against American and Filipino forces. MacArthur had been counting on air support from his B-17 bombers to help American and Filipino ground units, and with the loss of a significant amount of his aircraft prior to the invasion, the Japanese would have air superiority for the entirety of the invasion, which they used to devastating effect over the course of the six month campaign. As at Pearl Harbor, the Philippines campaign showed military planners in Washington how vital airplanes would be in the war.

Finally, by dispersing his ground forces to defend the entirety of the Philippines instead of immediately implementing WPO-3 to gather his troops at Bataan, MacArthur caused huge logistical problems and allowed the Japanese to encounter small groups of opposing troops instead of gathering all his forces together for a more concerted defense. Had his forces been able to move vital supplies to Bataan from the beginning, they could have put up a much stronger defense and would have stopped much of the suffering that American and Filipino troops experienced in the defense of Bataan later in the campaign.

Even with these mistakes in military strategy and execution, the fact of the matter was that the defense of the Philippines was a doomed task, and there was almost no way for MacArthur to hold off the Japanese invasion. Roosevelt's agreement to a Europe-first policy also meant that the Philippines were a secondary concern to military planners in Washington, so MacArthur's requests for additional troops and supplies would not be met. In fact, MacArthur's vocal statements about reinforcements, as well as his attempts to push American allies to attack Japanese forces in Asia, created conflicts within the army, and many military officials began to view MacArthur as a loose cannon that needed to be handled cautiously.

For the Japanese, the successful conclusion of the Philippines campaign was an important victory over the United States that showed their military prowess against a world power. However, looking more closely at their victory, the majority of the forces they faced were Philippine Army soldiers who were undertrained and poorly equipped. General Homma had also badly miscalculated in believing that MacArthur would try to defend Manila and that a decisive engagement would occur quickly in the campaign around the capital city. Instead, the decisive engagement occurred on the Bataan peninsula, and the American-Filipino defense at Bataan created major delays for Japanese expansion and especially forced them to commit more troops to the Philippines than they had wanted.

All told, the length of the Philippines campaign would have ripple effects in their ability to operate in other regions across the Pacific. Conquering the Philippines gave the Japanese a key piece to their plan of a Greater East Asia Co-prosperity Sphere, and it also gave the Japanese a resource-rich territory that would help them toward their goal of building an imperial network that would allow them to have a degree of resource self-sufficiency. On the other hand, the additional time they spent concentrating on the Philippines would hurt them just a few months later in the Pacific, especially after the decisive Battle of Midway proved to be a turning point in the war.

Bibliography

Buenafe, Manuel E. *Wartime Philippines*. Manila: Philippine Educational Foundation, 1950.
Chun, Clayton. *The Fall of the Philippines, 1941-42*. Oxford: Osprey Publishing, 2012.

Coleman, John S. *Bataan and Beyond: Memories of an American POW*. College Station and

London: Texas A&M University Press, 1978.

Falk, Stanley L. (1962). Bataan: The March of Death. New York: W. W. Norton & Company.

Harrison, Thomas R. (1989). SURVIVOR: Memoir of Defeat and Captivity – Bataan, 1942. Western Epics, Inc., Salt Lake City, Utah. ISBN 0-916095-29-0.

Jackson, Charles; Norton, Bruce H. (2003). I Am Alive!: A United States Marine's Story of Survival in a World War II Japanese POW Camp. Presidio Press. ISBN 0-345-44911-8.

Jansen, Marius B (2000). The Making of Modern Japan. Cambridge, MA: Harvard University Press. pp. 654–655. ISBN 978-0-674-00334-7. OCLC 44090600.

Knox, Donald. *Death March: The Survivors of Bataan*. New York and London: Harcourt Brace Jovanovich, Publishers, 1981.

Levering, Robert (1948). Horror trek; a true story of Bataan, the death march and three and one-half years in Japanese prison camps. Horstman Printing Co. ISBN 1258206307. OCLC 1168285.

Lukacs, John D. (2010). Escape from Davao. New York: Simon & Schuster. p. 433. ISBN 9780743262781. OCLC 464593097.

Machi, Mario (1994). Under the Rising Sun, Memories of a Japanese Prisoner of War. Wolfenden, USA. ISBN 0-9642521-0-4.

Masuda, Hiroshi (2012). MacArthur in Asia: The General and His Staff in the Philippines, Japan, and Korea. Ithaca, NY: Cornell University Press. ISBN 978-0-8014-4939-0.

Moody, Samuel B.; Allen, Maury (1961). Reprieve from Hell. New York: Pageant Press. OCLC 14924946.

Morrow, Don; Moore, Kevin (2011). Forsaken Heroes of the Pacific War: One Man's True Story. Roanoke, Virginia: Wounded Warrior Project. ISBN 978-1-56592-479-6. OCLC 725827438.

Murphy, Kevin. C. (2012). "'Raw Individualists': American Soldiers on the Bataan Death March Reconsidered". War & Society 31: 42–63. doi:10.1179/204243411X13201386799172. edit

Norman, Michael and Elizabeth Norman. *Tears in the Darkness: The Story of the Bataan Death March and its Aftermath*. New York: Farrar, Strauss and Giroux, 2009.
Quezon, Manuel Luis. *The Good Fight*. New York: Appleton-Century Co., 1974.

Resa, Jolinda Bull (2011). Honor Them Always: For the Sacrifice of Their Youth at Bataan. Outskirts Press, Inc. ISBN 978-1-4327-7555-1. OCLC 782073328.

Sides, Hampton (2001). Ghost Soldiers. New York: Anchor Books. ISBN 978-1299076518. OCLC 842990576.

Stephens, Harold (October 16, 1994). "Memories of the War". Humboldt Co., CA.: "Times-Standard," Sect. Style/potpourri.

Stewart, Sidney. Give Us This Day (revised ed.). W. W. Norton & Company. ISBN 0-393-31921-0.

Tenney, Lester (2000). My Hitch in Hell. Brassey's. ISBN 978-1574882988. OCLC 557622115.

Young, Donald J. (1992). The Battle of Bataan: A History of the 90 Day Siege and Eventual Surrender of 75,000 Filipino and United States Troops to the Japanese in World War. McFarland & Company. ISBN 0-89950-757-3.

The Philippines Campaign of 1944-1945

Chapter 1: Invasion Plan

The Philippines Campaign would be remembered as a decisive Allied victory and a personal vindication of sorts for Douglas MacArthur, but in 1943, it was still unclear whether the operation would ever take place. Military officials like General George C. Marshall, Lieutenant General Joseph McNarney, and General Henry Arnold all seemed to favor bypassing the Philippines for Formosa during late 1943 and early 1944, while others like Lieutenant General Brehon Somervell argued that it was important to take the entire Philippines before moving on to Formosa and China. For his part, MacArthur was very vocal in his belief that the American army and navy needed to liberate the Philippines before moving on to other portions of the plan.

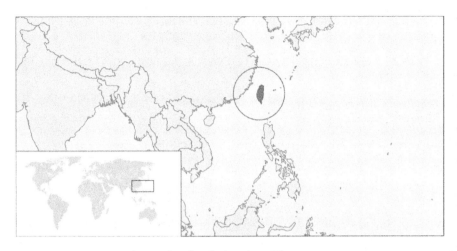

A map showing the location of Formosa

By March 1944, the Joint Chiefs decided to prepare for both options for the Allied attack and instructed MacArthur to prepare his men to move into the southern Philippines by the end of the year, and then into Luzon by early 1945. They also ordered Admiral Chester Nimitz to prepare for an assault on Formosa for early 1945.

Nimitz

Meanwhile, between March and June of 1944, American intelligence had learned that Japan was in the process of reinforcing areas under their control in the western Pacific, especially Formosa. This meant that the longer it took for the Americans to begin their attack on the island, the better-prepared Japanese forces would be to defend it. For the Joint Chiefs, this meant that in order to attack Formosa, they would have to move up their timetable to the fall of 1944 if they wanted to carry out an assault on the island.

Another complicating factor was the belief by American strategists that the Chinese resistance was in danger of collapsing against Japanese pressure. This would nullify one of the major reasons for privileging Formosa over the Philippines (aiding in the supply of Chinese forces on the mainland). By this time, both MacArthur and Nimitz were advocating the need to take the

Philippines to secure air bases from which the Allies could launch further operations across the Pacific. In July 1944, Roosevelt sailed to Pearl Harbor to discuss strategy. Although often cited as the key event in the lead up to the invasion of the Philippines, the truth is that the meeting was indecisive. It was not until September 1944 that President Roosevelt, the Joint Chiefs, MacArthur and Nimitz were all committed to the plan of invading the Philippines before engaging in further attacks on Japan. This made sense mostly in terms of aircraft ranges and the imperative to keep ground forces under the umbrella of short range fighters, but as MacArthur was soon to discover, the carriers were not up to the job on their own.

Once military leaders settled on the Philippines-first plan, they began to prepare for the upcoming campaign. The Allied strategy would comprise of four phases. First, naval and ground units would establish a foothold on southeastern Mindanao, where they could establish airfields that would support further operations. Next, Allied units would move into the central Philippines at Leyte, where MacArthur would set up air and supply bases for the attack on Luzon. The third phase involved taking Luzon, and then the fourth phase would involve dislodging Japanese troops from the minor Philippines islands that had been bypassed during the first three phases.

Ultimately, in September 1944, MacArthur revised the plan and eliminated the first phase at Mindanao, instead collapsing the plan into a three-phased assault that would begin at Leyte. Admiral William Halsey, in command of the U.S. 7th Fleet and directly subordinate to MacArthur, was a keen advocate of an attack on Leyte, a large island to the southeast of the Philippine archipelago. General Walter Krueger, commander of MacArthur's 8th army, was less enthusiastic. Buttressed by upbeat intelligence reports, MacArthur opted for Halsey's plan.

Halsey

Krueger

A problem that Allied forces encountered as they prepared for the Philippines invasion was Japanese reinforcements. Since Japanese military leaders were constantly moving troops and planes around, it became difficult for the Americans to estimate Japanese ground and aerial strength. For example, American leaders estimated that the Japanese had 400-500 planes in the Philippines, but that an additional 300-400 planes might be moved from Formosa, along with carrier-based planes that could be sent to the region to contest the American attack.

Chapter 2: Leyte and Mindoro

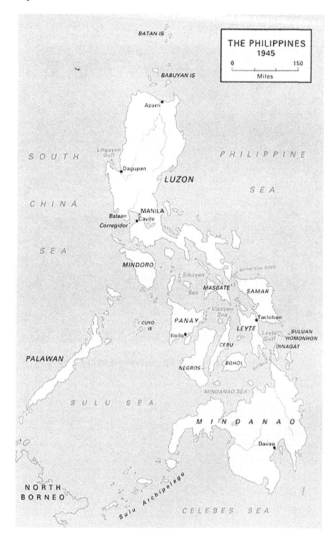

A map of the Philippines

MacArthur's forces began to fight for Leyte in late October 1944, and over the course of two months worth of fighting, the Allies eventually established themselves on the island and mostly wiped out the Japanese contingent, killing an estimated 50,000 Japanese. It was also at Leyte that the iconic picture of MacArthur wading ashore was taken, an image that has become closely associated with his return to the Philippines.

Picture of the amphibious invasion of Leyte

American soldiers fighting on Leyte

On the 23rd and 24th of October, the Imperial Japanese Navy made a desperate ride to Leyte Gulf, but luckily for MacArthur, they were completely overwhelmed by Nimitz's five task forces. For the first time, kamikaze attacks on shipping became commonplace, and the Japanese simultaneously poured ground and air reinforcements into Leyte. Although Nimitz had the better of the Imperial Fleet, he had his hands full, and this left MacArthur with inadequate cover from the American carriers, so it took his engineers much longer than expected to build airbases for his own fighters. Krueger's troops ran in to sustained resistance from the equivalent of five Japanese divisions, and it was not until the American 77th Division made an amphibious attack at Ormoc on December 7 and choked off Japanese supply that major combat operations on Leyte came to a close. As on New Guinea, MacArthur's garrisons had a great deal of fighting to do beyond that, mopping up pockets of resistance until May 1945. In a move not expected by MacArthur or Halsey, the Japanese had fought a major battle at Leyte. In doing so they had shocked and checked the Americans; but they had lost the remains of their battle fleet.

On December 12, 1944, MacArthur joined a very select club in receiving his fifth star. Like Ulysses S. Grant and Dwight Eisenhower, MacArthur was now a full General in the United States Army. Naturally, this did little to soften his self-esteem or moderate his optimism in military planning. When intelligence reports pitched Japanese numbers on Luzon at about a quarter of a million men, MacArthur dismissed the reports as "bunk". He had no rational basis for doing so whatsoever, and it's likely that his obsession with reaching Manila clouded his sober judgment. In fact, Japanese numbers would be much higher than estimated.

As MacArthur's campaign was progressing on Leyte, Allied forces began their attack on the Philippines with a landing at Mindoro, from which they planned to provide developed airfields that would allow them to give air cover to ships moving toward the Lingayen Gulf at Luzon. Secondarily, these airfields at Mindoro would give the Allies more options from which to contest Japanese air power in the region. American planners estimated the Japanese garrison on Mindoro to be roughly 1,000 men made up of a mix of the Japanese 8th Division and the 105th Division.

MacArthur assigned the American Sixth Army under General Krueger to carry out operations on Mindoro, and he would be supported by both air and naval units. Krueger delegated the task to Brigadier General William Dunckel, who utilized the 19th Regimental Combat Team of the 24th Division and the 503d Parachute RCT to carry out the mission. The ground forces began moving toward Mindoro on December 12, 1944 aboard the ships of Task Group 77.12. The Task Group moved unopposed through the Mindanao Sea until the next day, December 13, when they were spotted by Japanese surveillance. Japanese commanders held off attacking the Allied ships because they wanted to figure out the destination of the Task Group before engaging it, but by the middle of that afternoon, 10 Japanese plans, including three kamikaze planes, attacked the Task Group, with one kamikaze crashing into the flagship *Nashville*. With roughly 190 wounded sailors to deal with, some ships picked up survivors and returned to Leyte, while the command staff was transferred to the *Dashiell* to continue the mission.

Picture of a Japanese kamikaze plane during the campaign

Picture of an anti-aircraft crew on a Navy destroyer trying to cover Mindoro

By this time, the Japanese military believed the Task Group was headed toward either Panay, Cebu, or Negros, and in the course of searching for it near those areas, they wasted valuable time in which they could have continued their attacks. Meanwhile, on the morning of December 15, the Task Group reached Mindoro and began preparations for beach landings. As the landing units were disembarking, Japanese air operations attempted to aid ground troops in repelling the Allied forces. Although much of the Japanese air power was destroyed by Allied planes, kamikazes did manage to sink two landing ships, as well as the destroyer *Moale*. Japanese planes also damaged one other landing ship, the destroyer *Howorth*, and the CVE *Marcus Island*. In the air attacks, the Allies suffered 27 casualties, but aside from that, the troops of the 19th and 503d were able to land with little resistance, and this allowed some of the naval vessels of the Task Group to withdraw from the operation and move to support units in other locations.

As this was occurring, Allied planes attacked Luzon on December 16th, and the aircraft carriers designated for the Philippines campaign withdrew to the east for refueling before beginning a second series of attacks that took place on December 19th. Over the course of the next few days naval and aerial engagements with Japanese aircraft destroyed an estimated 450 enemy planes, leaving the Allies with almost complete air superiority over the Philippines until the Japanese called in reinforcements from Formosa and the home islands.

By December 15th, the 19th and 503d had created a beachhead seven miles inland at Mindoro and had taken the airfield at the town of San Jose. Army engineers who had accompanied the landing parties then began building new airstrips roughly three miles south of the airfield at San Jose. The new airstrips, at a site they called Hill Drome, became operational on December 20th, and on that day American P-38s and P-61s began arriving from elsewhere in the Pacific. These airfields would be important in opposing a Japanese counterattack, which began on December 20th when 50 Japanese planes flew in to reinforce the existing 15 planes the Japanese Army Air Force had at Mindoro. Air attacks on December 21st destroyed two more landing craft, and ground units stationed on Mindoro were also attacked, causing roughly 70 casualties.

To counter the Allies, Japanese commanders ordered their Southwestern Area Fleet, which was comprised of two cruisers and six destroyers and was stationed at Manila, to Mindoro on a raiding mission to try to sink Allied ships off the coast. However, the Southwester Area Fleet was spotted in the South China Sea by Allied submarines, and 105 planes were sent from Mindoro to engage with the fleet. Although the Southwestern Fleet was attacked from the air, they managed to make their way to the beachhead, where they shelled the beach and airfields for roughly 40 minutes before withdrawing. In total, the Southwestern Area Fleet managed to destroy 26 planes and damage some Allied installations on Mindoro, while suffering the loss of one destroyer and sustaining damage to nearly all of the ships in the fleet.

On December 28th, Japanese air attacks resumed against Allied naval units near Mindoro, where they sunk three ships, along with a tanker and two landing vessels. Although these were heavy losses for the Allied naval presence at Mindoro, the Japanese lost 50 aircraft between December 28th and January 4th, and with no more reinforcements forthcoming, Japanese air power in the region was once again basically nullified.

Meanwhile, on Mindoro proper, Allied ground units began patrols on December 19th, where they searched for Japanese troops and guarded areas that might be landing spots for reinforcements for the Japanese garrisons on Luzon. Mindoro guerrillas also worked with Allied troops by helping to guide the patrols and engaging some of the remaining Japanese soldiers in mopping-up operations across the island. Reinforcing the 19th and 503d, General Krueger sent the 21st Division to Mindoro after the Southwestern Fleet Raid just in case a ground-based attack was being planned by Japan.

Army engineers continued building on Mindoro, and MacArthur sent additional bombers and fighters to the air bases there in preparation for later missions. He also had engineers build airfields for heavy bombers that would target areas in the southern Philippines and Formosa. Work on these heavy bomber airfields began on January 2nd, but they would not be ready for heavy bomber support in time for the invasion of Luzon. Nonetheless, by the middle of January, Allied Air Forces had three fighter groups, two medium bomber groups, two night fighter squadrons, three tactical reconnaissance squadrons, a photographic squadron, and an air-sea rescue squadron. With this air power mustered at Mindoro, the principal goal of the invasion of the island of Mindoro was complete, as the Allies now had their air bases in which to launch further air attacks. They now also had a base close to Luzon that put pressure on the Japanese to defend multiple possible entry points onto that island.

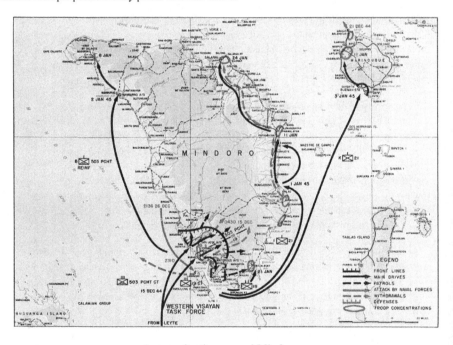

A map of action around Mindoro

Chapter 3: Moving Toward Luzon

With southern Mindoro under Allied control, MacArthur began a series of three feints to confuse Japanese forces on Luzon. First, he sent the Western Visayan Task Force to seize northeastern Mindoro and Marinduque Island, which he hoped would lead the Japanese to believe that the two areas would be bases from which the Allies would try to launch an invasion on southern Luzon. Then, naval units would begin fake maneuvers along the southern coast of Luzon, while guerrillas operating on Luzon would work with Allied forces in destroying infrastructure like railroads, bridges and communications lines in southern Luzon. Finally, Allied forces throughout the Pacific would maneuver to give the impression that Formosa, and not Luzon, was the next target for their operations.

On January 1st, the Western Visayan Task Force began its part of the operation by moving from its base in southern Mindoro toward northeastern Mindoro, which took them roughly 30 days to complete. As this was occurring, guerrilla operations in Mindoro had neutralized the remainder of the Japanese garrison on the island. These guerrillas killed 50 soldiers, and the remaining 300 stationed there fled into the interior.

However, the rest of the planned deception did not go as planned. The delays that the Western Visayan Task Force faced in moving to the north of the island meant that they did not arrive in time to put their part of the plan in place, but they did succeed in freeing groups of Filipinos on Mindoro. Nonetheless, Japanese commanders were well aware that Luzon was the next target of Allied operations, and that an attack would not occur in the southern region but instead would focus on the Lingayen Gulf, which was the same invasion point that the Japanese had used for its invasion back in 1941.

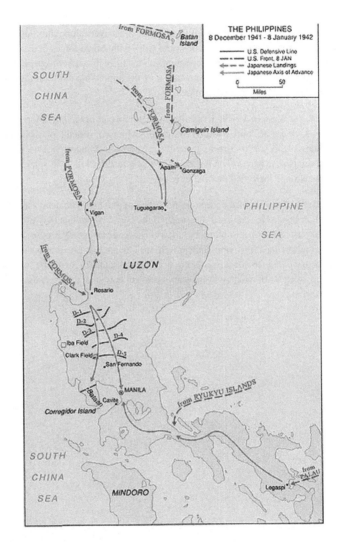

A map indicating the Japanese invasion points on Luzon in 1941

A picture of Filipino guerrillas on Mindoro

Allied aerial bombard of Luzon had begun in the fall of 1944, and they had already knocked out key military installations. Naval units also began to move on Luzon, with Admiral Halsey's carrier group and Admiral Kinkaid's surface forces nearing the Lingayen Gulf. In fact, during the beginning of the assault on Lingayen, military officials had problems coordinating staging activities between ground troops, naval vessels, and landing craft between the various launch and landing points. The initial landing at Lingayen Gulf involved two ground units, the XIV Corps and the I Corps. Along with these two ground units, the ships of the II and III Amphibious Force had the task of ferrying these units to their landing locations.

American battleships heading towards Lingayen Gulf

The landing units were designated the Luzon Attack Force, with the first group, consisting of screening and support ships, leaving from Leyte Gulf on January 2, 1945. Between January 4th and 5th, a second group left Leyte Gulf, this time consisting of three light cruisers, six destroyers, as well as smaller covering vessels. Finally, on January 6th, the ships carrying ground forces began making their way to the Lingayen Gulf.

To support this convoy of ships moving toward Lingayen Gulf, Mindoro-based planes began increasingly heavy attacks on Japanese targets in late December and early January. They especially targeted defensive installations at the Lingayen beaches, as well as Japanese transports bringing reinforcements to Luzon. The Third Fleet's fast carriers also moved into the region, and by January 3rd, they were in position to begin operations targeting Japanese air bases within range of Luzon: Formosa, the Ryukyu Islands, and the Pescadores. By January 6th, the fast carriers moved again, this time to the coast of Luzon, where they would provide cover over North Luzon (with Allied Air Force planes from Mindoro covering the Lingayen Gulf and Clark Field).

Picture of the Third Fleet moving towards the Philippines

In terms of the Japanese presence at Luzon by early January, 1945, when air attacks against island accelerated, they had only a minimal air presence remaining to contest the skies, so military leaders in Japan began to devote their resources to consolidating air power for the home islands rather than spreading out their remaining planes in an attempt to protect territories like the Philippines. The remaining Japanese planes at Luzon attempted a series of attacks on American naval units. They attacked a mine sweeping group off the coast of Mindoro and a kamikaze crashed into one ship, killing 95 men and wounding another 65. As these operations made clear, Japanese air tactics in their defense of the Philippines increasingly centered on the use of kamikazes, and on January 5th, planes attacked the Third Fleet, which was preparing for a new set of strikes on Luzon. Kamikaze planes hit two CVE, two heavy cruisers, three destroyers, a destroyer transport, and a mine sweeper, with total casualties for the day within the Third Fleet amounting to 65 dead and 195 wounded. On the other hand, the Japanese lost nearly all of the 45 planes that began the attacks, further depleting their already weak air forces.

At the same time, Japanese naval units also attempted to engage Allied forces. During the afternoon of January 5th, Allied ships spotted two Japanese destroyers that were attempting to attack a mine sweeper group near Manila Bay. A mixed group of two Australian frigates and an American destroyer attempted to intercept these ships, but when they were unable to get within firing range, they had to call off their attack plans and return to Manila Bay. Japanese submarines harassed other Allied naval vessels, with one group, which included the *Boise*, MacArthur's command ship, being fired upon by torpedoes. The torpedoes missed their marks, and one Japanese submarine was sunk by return fire.

At Lingayen Gulf, kamikaze planes were a major problem for Allied naval vessels. Admiral Jesse Oldendorf noted the problems he had in defending against kamikaze planes, as it only took one or two planes escaping away from Allied air cover to deal heavy damage to his ships. Anti-aircraft weapons were also problematic because their 5-inch antiaircraft weapons equipped with proximity fuses had problems tracking the erratic flight techniques of kamikaze pilots. Meanwhile, their 40 mm and 20 mm automatic batteries often did not deal enough damage to halt the heavily armored kamikaze planes. Fortunately, even though Allied forces had trouble dealing with kamikaze planes, the problem was lessened by the lack of aircraft that the Japanese on Luzon possessed. By January 6th, they had only a small number of operational planes remaining.

Oldendorf

Chapter 4: Luzon

A picture of the initial landings on Luzon

Allied soldiers advancing on Luzon

The plan for the Lingayen landings was to have 6th Army establish beachheads and then secure a base from which supplies and reinforcements could come ashore. They would then coordinate offensive maneuvers against the Japanese 14th Area Army. Thus, on January 9th, 1945, or S-day, the naval vessels positioned off the coast began their bombardment of potential Japanese positions at 0700. After half an hour, assault troops from the XIV Corps began coming ashore and were followed by the 37th Infantry Division, which landed to the XIV Corps' left, while the 40th Division landed on the right. The Japanese defenders did not contest the beaches here, and in fact, Filipino guerrillas began coming toward the American troops to help them.

By the evening of the 9th, some units had made their way as far as four miles into the interior of the island, but the next day, January 10th, saw some resistance from Japanese forces when a platoon of Japanese infantry attacked the 160th Division, which suffered 15 casualties, the most of any regiment in the first three days on Luzon. As they continued to move away from the beaches, with the 185th Infantry moving to the west and the 160th moving toward the south, a gap began to open between them. General Rapp Brush therefore moved the 108th Infantry to close this gap and stop a potential weak point in case of a Japanese counterattack.

Meanwhile, the 148th Infantry moved to the southeast, and with no resistance against it, quickly moved into its designated zone by the afternoon of January 10th. Nearby, the 129th Infantry made contact with Filipino guerrillas at the town of Malasiqui, and then later were attacked by Japanese units, forcing them to halt for the remainder of the day. Even with some slight delays, by January 11th, nearly all Allied assault units had reached their designated Army Beachhead Line zones, except on the right flank, where a series of hills and rough terrain made movement difficult.

The I Corps, which landed to the left of XIV Corps, was also able to complete their landings without any engagement by Japanese forces. The units that made up the I Corps included the 172nd Infantry, 1st and 3rd Battalions of the 43rd Division, and the 20th Infantry, along with the 6th Division being held in reserve, and they were able to move an average of three and a half miles in the first day. The 43rd Division of the I Corps had the most difficulty moving out from the beaches at Lingayen, as they had to travel over a series of hills whose compactness provided Japanese troops with natural cover from which to attack the Americans. As the 43rd Division's 169th Infantry moved to the southeast, they were attacked by Japanese mortar and artillery fire. The 169th Infantry was ordered to take Hill 470, one of the largest of the hill structure, but reconnaissance showed that the Japanese had strong defensive positions on that hill.

The 172nd Infantry also encountered artillery and mortar fire as it moved away from its landing location. Although harassed, they were able to quickly move away from the beaches and take their objective of Hill 247. On the next day, January 9th, the 103rd Infantry, was ordered to take Hill 200, a small cluster of hills on which the Japanese had built some defensive positions. Hill 200 was relatively geographically unimportant, but it blocked the most direct path to Route 3, a major north-south highway that led to Manila. The 103rd Infantry encountered sporadic attacks by small groups of Japanese troops that delayed their advance, and they were forced to halt for the night near the town of San Jacinto.

On January 10th, the 6th Division moved four miles inland, and by the time they stopped as night fell, they too had faced skirmishes with Japanese troops. Because of the harassment from Japanese units, these units within I Corps had fallen behind the scheduled pace, and now a gap appeared between XIV Corps and the I Corps. Another potential problem sprang up when the 103rd Infantry pursued and cleared nearby Japanese artillery pieces. This was an important task that neutralized their shelling of American troops in the area, but it opened another gap when the 103rd Infantry lost contact with the 6th Division on its right and the 169th Infantry, which was positioned to the left.

Also on the 10th, the 169th Infantry continued their attempt to take Hill 470, where they faced heavy resistance from Japanese units stationed there. The 169th battled their way forward and took the hill by the afternoon, and they were then ordered to take another area designated Hill 318, where they were pinned down by mortar and artillery fire. The 169th Infantry spent the rest of January 10th and January 11th dealing with the Japanese company that had dug in at Hill 318.

Another unit that was having problems advancing was the 172nd Infantry, also positioned on the left of the I Corps. Like the 169th, the 172nd had to face entrenched Japanese positions on hills that gave them the high ground on which to see American movements and position their artillery and mortars. While the Japanese soldiers did not directly engage the 172nd, they did target them with heavy shelling that made it difficult for the unit to progress. In fact, the 172nd Infantry was halted by Japanese shelling and had to be relieved by members of the Sixth Army Reserve on January 11th.

At MacArthur's headquarters, army commanders decided to commit the bulk of the Sixth Army Reserve to the I Corps, and to place them on the left flank, the only zone in which American troops were facing strong resistance from the Japanese. MacArthur came to believe that the Japanese had decided not to contest the beach landings and had withdrawn into the interior in an attempt to lure the Americans into a false sense of security and to overextend them, which would allow for a counterattack by Japanese units. He felt that on the left of I Corps, his troops had made contact with the forward Japanese defensive lines, and that they would have to be careful in advancing from this point on.

As MacArthur focused his attention on the left, he sent reconnaissance missions and made contact with Filipino guerrillas who provided information on Japanese troop movements. These sources painted a picture of the Japanese holding positions to the north and east of the I Corps landing sites, and the engagements that had occurred on January 10th and 11th were designed to slow the American drive to give Japanese forces from elsewhere on the island time to gather and prepare for a counterattack.

The Japanese 14th Area Army, under the command of General Tomoyuki Yamashita, was aware of the imminent American invasion, and that it would occur through Lingayen Gulf, but the Japanese did not expect it to occur as soon as it did. Japanese commanders had originally planned to make a decisive stand at Luzon, but when the Americans invaded Leyte, they decided to commit to a major engagement there. Leyte was a complete disaster for the Japanese, and the significant losses they faced there directly impacted their ability to defend Luzon later on in the war. Three divisions were diverted from Leyte in late fall of 1944 to aid in the defense of Luzon, but Allied air and naval attacks sunk transports that cost the Japanese nearly a third of their reinforcements and a large quantity of supplies. Yamashita had been planning to use his reinforcements to mount a counterattack shortly after the Americans landed, but with the losses that these divisions faced in transport to Luzon, he decided instead on drawing up defensive lines and holding out for as long as possible.

Yamashita

Like the American defense of Luzon in 1941, Yamashita and the 14th Area Army faced shortages of food, ammunition and medical supplies that would greatly impact their ability to hold out. In fact, by mid-November 1944, even before the American landings, food shortages were so dire that many soldiers had their rations cut by one-third. Also mirroring the American defense of Luzon, Yamashita decided against defending Manila and instead moved supplies away from the city for a more decentralized defense of the island. Japanese troop strength was very poor, as divisions were hastily formed from garrison units, as well as sailors stationed on the island and even Japanese civilians. Regular units were also in poor condition and lacked equipment. This would play a heavy role in Yamashita's ability to defend Luzon in the face of the American advance.

Unlike MacArthur in 1941-1942, Yamashita did not plan to withdraw into the Bataan peninsula, which he felt was too compact an area in which to mount a defense with the 275,000 soldiers that were available to him. Instead, he decided to leave the southern portion of the Lingayen Gulf undefended, where the terrain was too flat to mount a serious defense, so he gathered his troops to the north and east, where the hills and mountains that made up that zone would allow him to create strong defensive positions. For this, he created a special force called the Shobu Group, whose 152,000 troops were ordered to hold the hills and mountains in the area.

Yamashita also decided to defend a second area, a mountainous region near Clark Field in the Central Plains. His goal here was to stop Allied forces from being able to use the main airfield in Luzon for as long as possible. The soldiers sent to this area were called the Kembu Group, and numbered roughly 30,000 men, but were composed of a mix of army engineers, airplane ground crews, and antiaircraft units, in addition to experienced soldiers.

Yamashita set up a third major force called the Shimbu Group, which was ordered to defend the mountains to the north and east of Manila. The Shimbu Group was supposed to help facilitate the removal of supplies from Manila, and once this had been accomplished, they were ordered to destroy major roads and bridges surrounding the city. The Shimbu Group consisted of roughly 80,000 men.

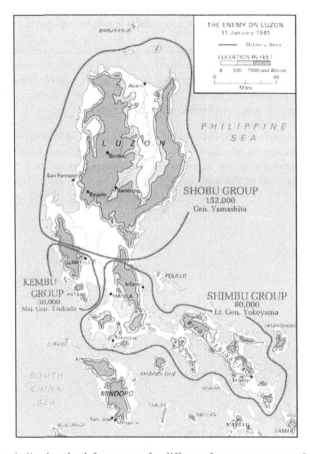

A map indicating the defense zones for different Japanese groups on Luzon

The Japanese soldiers who made contact with American troops after the Lingayen landings were members of the Shobu Group, and these soldiers had created a triangular defensive perimeter among the mountains of northern Luzon. Their goal was to hold the roads leading to the Cagayan Valley until the Japanese could move supplies out of the valley. Yamashita deployed reconnaissance units to patrol along the southern shores of the Lingayen Gulf with orders to withdraw if they encountered any resistance, but some units were caught out of position during the Allied landings, and these were the Japanese soldiers who the American I Corps first made contact with.

On January 11th, the I Corps began moving north hoping to capture the junction of Routes 3 and 11, which would secure the left flank and would allow the Sixth Army to begin its drive toward Manila without fear of counterattacks from this area. This important junction was defended by the Japanese 58th IMB, which had taken the high ground and had constructed a number of trenches and tunnels along the area's hills. There were 6,900 soldiers in the 58th IMB, and they also had 15 75 mm guns and 12 artillery pieces to help them in their defense. The American advance troops, composed of the 158th RCT with about 4,500 men, were tasked with making contact with the 58th IMB and would then have the help of nearby planes and ships, which would bombard the Japanese positions before a ground assault.

On January 12th, the 172nd Infantry began an attack on Hill 580, which was a Japanese advanced position located four miles away from the junction. Their first attempt on the hill was unsuccessful, and it would take until the next day before they were able to overcome the Japanese troops defending it. Once Hill 580 was captured, the 172nd continued forward with help from the 43rd Division's 103rd Field Artillery Battalion, and they captured Hill 565 before moving to within two and a half miles of the main Japanese position at the junction of Routes 3 and 11. A second operation involving the 63rd and 158th Infantry Regiments engaged nearby Japanese fortified positions, but problems with their artillery support delayed their movement, and the 63rd Infantry had problems linking up with the 158th Infantry at the designated point near Routes 3 and 11.

On January 14th, the 158th Infantry was surprised by the Japanese 58th IMB, allowing the Japanese to deal heavy damage with their artillery pieces. Japanese troops had also been able to hide from American patrols in the network of caves and tunnels they had dug, and since the Americans had no idea that this Japanese position stood in their way, they inflicted 85 more casualties. The next day, the 158th called in air and naval support, which allowed them to advance about 1,000 yards. At the same time, the 63rd Infantry, positioned to the east of the 158th, was also taking heavy fire from Japanese artillery positions.

By January 15th, American commanders realized that both the 158th and 63rd were facing much stronger Japanese positions than they had originally believed, and therefore General Leonard Wing redirected the 172nd Infantry to flank the Japanese by coming through the town of Rosario and then attacking Japanese artillery positions on the north of Route 3 from behind. He also sent some troops from the 169th Infantry to bolster these forces. However, even with the new troops moving into the area, Allied forces were unable to dislodge the Japanese from their strong defensive positions among the hills near the Route 3 and 11 junction, and a stalemate developed that halted all progress along the 43rd Division's left.

Along the right, the 103rd and 169th Infantry Regiments were driving eastward. By January 13th, they had reached the Japanese 23rd Division's outer defense perimeter, and they began operations to take two major points along this outer perimeter: Hill 319 and Hill 355. The 169th Infantry attacked the Japanese 64th Infantry, whose orders were to hold the western approaches to

Route 3. The 64th Infantry held the high ground on Hill 318, which allowed them to observe all activities by the Allied forces and utilize excellent artillery placement for their defense of the hill. The 169th Infantry was ordered to embark on a frontal assault of Hill 318, which they accomplished at the cost of 70 casualties. From the first few days on Luzon, American commanders realized that the time-consuming nature of assaults on dug-in Japanese hill-top positions meant that a rapid advance onto Route 3 was probably impossible, and so General Wing ordered the 169th Infantry to go around Hill 355 rather than attack it and instead move through the town of Palacpalac.

The 103rd Infantry was ordered to take a Japanese position south of the 169th's position called Hill 200. Hill 200 was another Japanese perimeter position in which they linked a series of hills by building tunnels and caves. As at other similar locations, aerial bombardment did little damage to these positions because Japanese troops could hide in the caves to avoid most bombs. This meant that the 103rd had to painstakingly clear Hill 200, beginning on January 12th. Hill 200 was only manned by 400 Japanese soldiers, but it took about four days to completely take the hill, and by the night of January 16th, the Americans had just concluded mopping up operations when they were attacked by a force of Japanese tanks moving in from the east. The Japanese counterattack was not a large-scale concerted effort to push out against Allied troops but merely consisted of a series of smaller counterattacks that Yamashita allowed his subordinates to engage in. Yamashita wanted to avoid the possibility of losing a large number of soldiers in one engagement, but he also wanted to delay the Allied advance.

In this series of counterattacks, the Japanese 71st Infantry attacked the rear of the Allied 172nd and 169th Infantry Regiments, while the Japanese 72nd Infantry attacked the rear of the Allied 169th and 103rd Infantry Regiments. As this was occurring, the 23rd Division sent a tank-infantry force to stop the advance of the Allied 103rd Infantry. Although the Japanese 71st and 72nd were able to get to the rear of the Allied positions, they were quickly pushed back.

At Palacpalac, 200 Japanese soldiers came into contact with the 1st Battalion of the 169th Infantry during the night of January 16th. Both groups were surprised by the attack, as the Japanese did not expect to see American soldiers at that location. The ensuing engagement lasted until the night of the 17th, and the 169th suffered 30 casualties in the fighting. The largest of the series of counterattacks occurred with the Shigemi Detachment attacking the 3rd Battalion of the 103rd Infantry. During nighttime on January 16th, Japanese tanks and infantry attacked an American position near the town of Potpot, and two Japanese tanks broke through the perimeter while a third was destroyed by antitank fire. The accompanying Japanese infantry then engaged in a two-hour battle with American soldiers before finally withdrawing. The two tanks that had broken through the line later returned in the early morning hours of January 17th, where they were engaged by American troops and destroyed. In this battle, the Americans suffered 12 casualties and lost one 37 mm antitank gun, a jeep, a scout car, and a tank. The Japanese lost 11 tanks in the engagement, as well as 50 soldiers killed.

By sunrise on January 17th, the Japanese counterattacks had ended and American commanders began reinforcing their forward positions (the 169th and 103rd Infantry Regiments). On the 17th, American forces held a 25 mile wide front that included some important Japanese perimeter defense positions, but even with these gains, the 43rd Division still had important work to do in its sector of the front. They needed to take the junction connecting Routes 3 and 11, and then they needed to push through to the southern portion of Route 3, which was an important road for Japanese movements of supplies and troops. Making things more difficult, as of January 17th, the 43rd Division had seen the bulk of fighting against the Japanese and had suffered roughly 800 casualties up to that point.

The 43rd Division, along with its reinforcements from the 158th and 63rd Infantry Regiments, began moving toward the Route 3 and 11 junction, which was being defended by the Japanese 58th IMB and 23rd Division, which held territory south of the junction. Japanese forces observed as American troops began moving toward their positions and did not engage as the Americans took control of the junction; instead, they allowed American forces to continue moving south of the junction to a defensive complex called Hill 35-Mt. Alava, which they had heavily fortified. The American 169th Infantry, meanwhile, probed the area for new approaches to Hill 355 and Mt. Alava while one battalion was posted near Hill 355 in order to keep Japanese units from counterattacking from that position.

The 169th Infantry spent January 17th and 18th preparing to attack Mt. Alava from the east and southeast. On the 18th the 2nd Battalion scouted new approaches to the Japanese position before moving past the town of Sison by midday, but in the late afternoon, Japanese forces began firing mortars and artillery at the 169th, pinning the American troops down near the town. On the 19th, some units of the Japanese 64th Infantry began withdrawing to Mt. Alava to attack the 169th Infantry's 2nd Battalion from the southwest, and by midday on the 19th, Japanese artillery and ground troops forced American troops to withdraw in the face of heavy fire. Since the Americans had to withdraw on flat land with no protection, they faced casualties of nearly half their troop strength (350 combat-ready men out of an initial force of 1,000), but they were eventually able to link up with the 716th Tank Battalion near Route 3, which forced the Japanese to call off their pursuit. The Japanese 64th Infantry at Mt. Alava also took heavy losses in the engagement, as they had compromised their defensive positions in the attack and roughly 400 of their men had been killed in the process of forcing an American retreat. Mt. Alava was now in a precarious position, and when the Americans launched an attack on Japanese defenses there on January 20th, they were able to overcome the small force still stationed there, taking the crest of the mountain by late afternoon and finishing up operations by the 21st.

Having taken one of the key points in the area, American forces now began preparations to take Hill 355, which they had initially isolated and bypassed. During January 22nd and 23rd, American troops engaged in a series of assaults on the hill against dogged resistance from Japanese soldiers, but by late on the 24th, American troops had finally taken most of Hill 355, killing 500 Japanese soldiers from the 64th Infantry in the process. Mopping up operations continued until January 28th as American units continued to engage the last remaining clusters of Japanese troops on Hill 355, killing 150 and capturing an assortment of artillery and antitank guns. By January 29th, after having wiped out Japanese troops at both Hill 355 and Mt. Alava, the 169th Infantry returned to join up with the other American forces in the area.

As the 169th Infantry was engaging Japanese troops on Mt. Alava and Hill 355, the 103rd Infantry began operations nearby at Pozorrubio. The 103rd began by attacking Hill 600, an elevated area between Pozorrubio and the Routes 3 and 11 junction. The 103rd attacked through frontal assaults on the Japanese positions, gaining some ground on the hill, but they were unable to overcome Japanese defenses. On January 22nd, after the attack had been ongoing for a few days, a group of officers was meeting at a forward area on Hill 600 when they were hit by Japanese artillery fire. The unit lost four company commanders and 2 other officers, as well as 7 enlisted men, with 33 other soldiers injured in the attack. This forced the 103rd Infantry to retreat from their positions on Hill 600, and American strategists decided to regroup and plan a new strategy against Hill 600 and other nearby hills.

General Wing began by deploying the 103rd Infantry to attack Hill 600 from the northwest before moving on to Hill 800. The 169th Infantry moved up to the north of the 103rd, where they would take Question Mark Hill, located near Hill 800. Finally, the 63rd Infantry, which had previously been held back as I Corps reserves, was deployed to take Benchmark Hill, located northwest of Question Mark Hill. The operation began on January 25th and continued until January 27th as American troops engaged in a series of frontal assaults on Japanese positions. The 3rd Battalion, 63rd Infantry attacked from the west side of Benchmark Hill and were able to secure it after taking 36 casualties. They then joined the rest of the 63rd Infantry to clear Hill 1500.

The 169th Infantry attacked Question Mark Hill and were able to take most of the hill, but they could not dislodge the Japanese soldiers fighting on the eastern side of the hill. On the 27th, they changed tactics and brought artillery and bombers to attack the remaining Japanese troops on that hill. The 103rd Infantry moved against Japanese positions on Hill 700 and Hill 600 on January 25th, but they were pushed back by intense Japanese fire against their attacks. Late in the afternoon, members of the 103rd found an undefended area connecting the two hills, and they were able to use this area to launch renewed attacks that surprised the Japanese defenders, allowing the Americans to take both hills.

As I Corps was pushing forward, XIV Corps was moving through the Central Plains, where up to January 18th they had suffered few casualties. General Oscar Griswold, XIV Corps commander planned to push his troops forward in a series of controlled advances to make sure they kept their supply line secured and did not outrun I Corps. Their continued lack of engagement with Japanese forces meant that the XIV Corps moved quickly through January 21st until its forward elements created a perimeter line south of the towns of Victoria and Tarlac. Tarlac especially had been an important railroad junction for the Japanese, who had stored a large quantity of supplies there, and Allied bombers had hit Tarlac heavily in the buildup to the landings, so when the forward units of the XIV Corps arrived, the Japanese garrison had withdrawn into the interior of Luzon and the town itself was badly damaged.

Griswold

Encountering no resistance from Japanese troops, the XIV Corps advanced past the Victoria-Tarlac line, and with the speed at which they were advancing, General Griswold was instructed to take Clark Air Field. Even though his troops had not faced significant Japanese opposition, Griswold was worried about the speed with which the XIV Corps was advancing. At one level, he believed he was stretching his supply lines thin, which would be a big problem if his troops later faced Japanese counterattacks, and he was also concerned that a gap had opened between the XIV Corps and the I Corps, which meant his left flank was exposed between the towns of Cuyapo and La Paz. Griswold had received vague reports of Japanese troops movements near Cabanatuan, 15 miles east of La Paz, and American patrols in the following days came into contact with Japanese troops at Moncada and La Paz. During the night of January 21-22, a platoon of Japanese infantry, in concert with one tank, attacked the 148th Infantry's perimeter one mile west of La Paz. The Japanese withdrew after destroying a bridge in the area.

American commanders decided to shore up the area between I Corps and XIV Corps by having the 37th Division and 40th Division move into the XIV Corps' left, where they would also float into the I Corps sector, thus filling the gap between the two forces. During the evening of January 22nd, the advanced elements of the 160th Infantry, along with the 40th Reconnaissance Troop, reached Capas, where they nearly came upon the Japanese garrison stationed there. The Japanese just managed to evade an attack, hurriedly escaping while leaving supplies behind. The next day, on the 40th Reconnaissance's left, the 108th Infantry came across some Japanese soldiers who had not retreated in time from the towns surrounding Capas and engaged them. On the right, the bulk of the 160th Infantry advanced unopposed to take Bamban Airfield, while one battalion of the 160th was tasked with securing the town of Bamban, where they fought with Japanese soldiers defending the town. It took them most of the day to secure the town, but once this was accomplished, they rejoined with the rest of the 160th and moved toward a network of ridges to the west of the town, where they were engaged by Japanese positions utilizing small arms fire and mortars.

This strong Japanese position surprised American commanders, who believed that the main Japanese defense of the area would be centered on Clark Field. After halting and gathering his forces, General Griswold had the 160th Infantry engage the Japanese defenses while the 40th Division probed for Japanese positions to the west and southwest, the direction of Clark Field. He also kept the 37th Division and 129th RCT in reserve to help in the push forward if needed. The problem Griswold faced in confronting Japanese defenses was that the Americans had little information about Japanese troops strength in this area. War planners estimated that there were between 4,000 and 8,000 Japanese soldiers around Clark Field, and American intelligence believed most of these troops were members of the Air Force, meaning only a few soldiers would be experienced in ground combat. American military officials therefore believed that there would only be weak resistance to the American advance at Clark Field.

In actuality, the Japanese stationed the Kembu Group at Clark Field, which was composed of 15,000 men from the Army and Navy. Of these 15,000 men, roughly 8,500 were experienced ground combat soldiers split into four units defending the area surrounding Clark Field, and the Japanese defenses protected not only Clark Field but also the route south toward Manila. The American 40th Division, which probed Japanese defenses to the west and southwest, made contact with enemy positions on January 23rd and then began an attack against them, but American soldiers encountered problems with the landscape as they had to climb hills devoid of any kind of protection while facing machine gun and mortar fire. The unit attacking what was called Hill 1800 was able to overcome Japanese defenses, but on the next hill, Hill 500, American soldiers were unable make any progress up the slope against intense Japanese fire.

Even with a detachment of the 40th Division being stopped at Hill 500, American commanders still believed that they were encountering a small defensive force rather than the Kembu Group's defensive perimeter, so they believed American forces could quickly overcome the defenses and take Clark Field. On January 25th, the 160th Infantry attacked Hill 636, overcoming one defensive position before meeting heavy resistance halfway up the hill. To the north, other members of the

160th attacked other hills in the area, first taking Hill E before attacking Japanese defenses on Hill G. Even though Japanese defenses were much heavier than the Americans had planned for, their attacks took a heavy toll on the Japanese center and the 160th Infantry was threatening to outflank Japanese positions on their right. While the Japanese expected their defenses to hold for at least a week, they were already in danger of being overrun in the first few days of fighting.

Griswold next ordered the 160th and 108th Infantry Regiments to move toward the south and attack Hill 636, which blocked the path to Clark Field. Once they overcame defenses at Hill 636, they could secure Clark Field and then move toward nearby Fort Stotsenburg. As was the case in nearly all American attacks on Japanese hilltop defensive positions, Japanese troops fired machine gun, artillery, and mortar rounds at American soldiers, pinning them down and forcing them to call for mortar and artillery support. American fire then allowed the ground troops to move forward a bit at a time until they could take a Japanese machine gun or artillery position before having to repeat the process. This meant that the process of overcoming Japanese defenses was painstaking and slow, with each American battalion involved in the fighting losing an average of 20 casualties per day. At the same time, while Japanese soldiers slowly wore down American units, they were unable to halt the slow and steady gains that American troops made day after day.

On January 26th, the 160th Infantry made a big push on the Japanese right, taking Hill 636 and Hill 600 against soldiers who were unable to hold their positions and had to retreat in the face of the American attack. Meanwhile, the 108th Infantry attacked closer to the center, where Japanese defenses held and stalled their progress. By this time, American commanders had realized they were up against strong Japanese defenses and scrapped their plans for a quick victory at Clark Field. Even though their progress was slowed by the stronger Japanese defenses, as of January 27th, they had dealt damage to Japanese positions and had also captured major transportation points at the Manila Railroad and Route 3 near the town of Bamban. Japanese forces were also suffering heavy losses, with the Takayama Detachment of the Kembu Group alone losing nearly 1,000 men killed in the fighting up to this point.

On January 28th, the 40th Division began a new attack against the Kembu Group's positions, with the 129th Infantry coming in from the west with support from the 754th Tank Battalion. To the north, the 160th Infantry gained quite a bit of territory near Hill 620 before getting pinned down by gunfire and artillery. They were later hit by a counterattack that pushed them backward. On the 29th, the 160th Infantry regrouped and broke through the center of the Takaya Detachment's position.

The 129th Infantry also saw major action when they were ordered to take a Japanese hill-position called Top of the World. This location was a strongly defended, 1,000 foot high hill that was the major objective in the area. The 1st Battalion, 129th Infantry began the attack on the morning of January 31st, where they were quickly pinned down by enemy fire, but the 1st

Battalion was ultimately able to make some headway during the afternoon, and by nightfall, they had gained a precarious foothold halfway up the hill. On February 1st, more units of the 129th climbed the hill, and after fierce fighting, they were able to take the crest by midday.

The result of these engagements on the right led to huge losses for the Kembu Group. American troops had penetrated areas along the flanks and center of their position and had also effectively destroyed the armored units that were attached to the group. Over 2,500 Japanese soldiers had been killed or injured, and a further 750 casualties had occurred among reinforcements that had been sent to aid the Kembu Group. By early February, the XIV Corps had taken Clark Field and had secured critical areas of Route 3 and the Manila Railroad. This meant that while the Kembu Group was still a threat, they had been sufficiently weakened that the Americans could begin to turn their attention toward Manila.

Pictures of abandoned Japanese planes at Clark Field

Chapter 5: Advancing to Manila

At San Jose, roughly 100 miles north of Manila, along with the towns of Lupao and Munoz, Japanese commanders placed the 10th and 105th Divisions, along with the 2nd Tank Division. These units were reinforced by the 7th and 10th Tank regiments and the 2nd Mobile Infantry. These would be the troops tasked with opposing the I Corps as it moved south. For the I Corps, their plan of attack against San Jose involved a pincer maneuver, with an attack from the northeast through Munoz being carried out by the 6th Division while the 25th Division would attack from the southeast through Lupao.

The drive toward San Jose began on February 1st, and the I Corps would have to cross flat land with little cover against a defense that consisted of dug-in Japanese medium tanks, with support from infantry units and machine gun positions. The 3rd Battalion, 20th Infantry led the line, and they were confronted by Japanese tanks and artillery south of Route 99, the road leading into Munoz. On the 2nd, the 1st Battalion, 20th Infantry again was halted by the Japanese defense, while the 2nd Battalion also failed to make much headway against Japanese defenses near Route 5. The 1st Battalion, 35th Infantry advanced close to Lupao before taking artillery, mortar and machine gun fire from Japanese defenses in the town. This forced the 1st Battalion to retreat, and on the next day they resumed the attack but were unable to make gains, and like the 20th Infantry, were unable to take their town.

Because of the slow progress, American commanders decided to bypass both towns, thus sending reinforcements to keep Japanese forces confined within Lupao and Munoz while the main body of troops moved forward toward their objectives. The 35th Infantry, along with the 6th Division, advanced near San Jose, and on February 4th, they were able to take the town almost unopposed. With that, American commanders realized that the Japanese had committed the bulk of their forces to defending the paths leading into San Jose at Munoz and Lupao, and had virtually no remaining troops to defend San Jose proper. The Japanese troops remaining in these towns were increasingly isolated and surrounded by American units, and the Japanese defenders at Munoz attempted to break out on February 7th. They failed to realize that Route 5, their escape path away from town, was in the hands of the Americans, and they were quickly engaged by strong American positions along the road that virtually wiped them out.

At Lupao, the 35th Infantry advanced, pushing Japanese troops further and further back until they too decided to attempt a break out. A group of 11 tanks attempted to break through the 35th Infantry's line, and five of them were able to get away. Their crews left the tanks in the foothills near town and retreated on foot. Japanese infantrymen also retreated away from the town, and by February 8th, American troops held Lupao.

Across the Central Plains, the 40th Division continued fighting the Kembu Group in mid-February, and American units continued to deal with the difficult task of assaulting dug-in Japanese troops. The XIV Corps had taken Clark Field and controlled an important point in the Japanese defenses at Top of the World, but the Kembu Group still had roughly 25,000 soldiers holding strong positions in the foothills near the Bamban River. For General Krueger and the XIV Corps, the task of defeating the Kembu Group would involve coordinated attacks involving air support and artillery fire that would force the Japanese troops into their trenches and caves for protection, which would be followed by American infantry operations.

On February 6th, General Kruger ordered the XIV Corps to re-engage the Kembu Group. The plan of attack involved the 185th and 160th Infantry Regiments attacking the center of the Kembu Group's position, while the 108th moved on the right and the 129th on the left. On February 6th, the 160th Infantry began operations against McSevney Point, a major defensive position for Japanese troops. The 160th was aided by support from tanks, planes, and artillery, which pinned down Japanese troops in their foxholes and caves as American infantry advanced behind them to attack the enemy troops as they emerged from their shelters. It took three days for the 160th to take the summit of McSevney Point, followed by a series of ferocious Japanese night counterattacks. On the morning of February 10th, the 160th realized that the Japanese had withdrawn from the position following their last unsuccessful counterattack.

The loss of McSevney Point convinced the commander of the Kembu Group to withdraw from that portion of the defense perimeter to their last-stand positions, which created a gap in the defensive line that isolated the two wings. The gaps created by this maneuver allowed American units on both flanks to drive the Japanese troops back. On the Japanese right, the Eguchi-Yanagimoto Detachment held out for nearly a week, but by February 12th, they had lost everything except Hill 7. With that detachment defeated at Hill 7 on the afternoon of the 12th, the 108th Infantry had overcome the Japanese right.

On the left, the 185th Infantry was making important gains against the Japanese defenses, while in the center the 160th Infantry had pushed forward into the Japanese's last-stand line. American units continued moving forward in the painstaking task of taking hill after hill, and between February 10 and 12, American troops took three of the last major Japanese hill positions. On February 15th, with continued American advances on the left, right and center, and with heavy casualties among its soldiers, the Kembu Group was effectively destroyed. Isolated units of the Kembu Group still remained, but the XIV Corps now only needed to engage in mop-up operations, and American commanders could fully turn their attention to the drive to Manila. Overall, the XIV Corps lost 285 men killed and 1,180 wounded, while the Kembu Group suffered 12,000 deaths (Smith, p.206)

The rest of XIV Corps had been moving toward Manila since late January. While they were harassed by Japanese units during this time, they were not appreciably slowed in their drive toward the capital, and by early February, American commanders had planned for a pincer maneuver involving the XIV Corps from the north and the 11th Airborne Division moving in from the south. The 11th Airborne landed in southern Luzon on January 31st at Nasugbu, a site that allowed them to isolate Japanese forces in southern Luzon (so they would not be able to reinforce defenses at Manila) and position themselves for the drive north to that city.

After landing, the 11th Airborne's 511th Infantry led the line in moving north to Manila, but they were delayed when they had to fight a series of actions against small Japanese units defending the bridges leading to the capital city. In fact, the major obstacle for the 11th Airborne involved the logistics of their movement, as Japanese destruction (and attempted destruction) of bridges challenged their ability to move men and supplies to their staging points for the attack on Manila. Army engineers had to work quickly, using pontoons and reinforcing roads and undamaged bridges to keep the 11th Airborne moving.

Chapter 6: Taking Manila

There were roughly 10,000 Japanese troops stationed at Manila, and they were broken up into three combat groups that defended the north, south, and center of the city. However, aside from breaking their troops up into these groups, the plan for defending the city was not well-conceived, with Japanese officers looking to inflict heavy casualties on American troops and to stop them from controlling Manila for as long as possible. They also planned to demolish infrastructure that could be useful to the Americans, such as the port area, bridges, water supply system and power grid. Japanese troops cannibalized guns from wrecked aircraft and ships, and many of their heavier weapons were 20-mm and 25-mm airplane guns that were modified for use on the ground.

The XIV Corps reached the outskirts of Manila on February 3rd and promptly began operations against the suburb of Santo Tomas, where the 8th Cavalry experienced the first instance of close-quarter city fighting in Manila when they were attacked by Japanese troops hiding in buildings at the intersection of Quezon Boulevard. The Japanese hid among numerous buildings, including Bilibid Prison and Far Eastern University. The 8th Cavalry was able to retreat away from the intersection, and while there was potential for heavy fighting at Santo Tomas, this did not materialize because Japanese troops stationed there were surprised by the American advance and had not expected their arrival for another two weeks. Thus, the Japanese units stationed there retreated following the engagement at Quezon Boulevard and the Americans were able to take control of the suburb.

Along with the 8th Cavalry, the 37th Division made its way into the city from the north, and its 145th Infantry began clearing the Tonto District, which they accomplished on the morning of February 9th. To the left of the Tonto District, the 148th Infantry cleared the Binondo District before moving on to the Santa Cruz District. As this was occurring, Japanese troops in the area blew up the Pasig-Jones and Santa Cruz Bridges, the two western bridges into the city. The Japanese Northern Force also began destroying military stores and installations along the northern entrance to the city, setting off large-scale fires that were intensified by strong winds. These fires lasted until February 6th before they were finally brought under control by American troops and Filipino citizens.

Aside from the fires, the 37th Division and 1st Cavalry Division had little problem clearing the northern suburbs of Japanese forces. In fact, the Northern Force had executed its orders to destroy certain key points and had withdrawn south over the Pasig River, where they destroyed the bridges after they had crossed. American troops killed roughly 1,500 Japanese soldiers in various engagements throughout the northern sector prior to the withdrawal, and this had given the Americans experience in what to expect in the fighting to follow.

On the morning of February 7th, the 37th Division was ordered across the Pasig River, where they would engage the Central Force's 1st Naval Battalion in the western portion of Paco District, and especially Provisor Island. The 37th Division had no problems making their way to Paco District, but upon reaching the Paco Railroad Station, they faced heavy fighting from Japanese troops stationed there, as well as those in the nearby buildings of Concordia College and Paco

School. On the night of February 9th, most of the Japanese troops withdrew from these positions, and when the 148th Infantry stormed the Japanese positions the next day, they faced a much smaller force than expected.

Meanwhile, the 129th Infantry crossed the Pasig on February 8th and then moved west toward Provisor Island. A small force in two boats tried to sneak across the river to the island to take one of the outbuildings and create a landing spot for the invasion of the island, but they were quickly attacked by Japanese troops and were only saved from being wiped out because of mortar support that kept Japanese troops from surrounding them. That night, they were evacuated off the island, but the force had sustained 17 casualties in the aborted mission. The next day, the 129th fired artillery and mortar rounds at the island to soften up defenses for another attempted amphibious landing, this time involving 90 men. Three boats were sunk by machine gun and mortar fire, but the rest were able to make it to the island, where they took the boiler building while mortar and artillery fire pounded the rest of the island. The mortar and artillery fire dealt heavy damage to Japanese positions, and American troops were able to secure the island on February 11th. Their goal in taking the island was to control the power plant located there to provide power for the city, but the Japanese troops had destroyed some of the equipment prior to the American landings, so they were unable to use the power plant.

The 1st Cavalry was ordered across the Pasig River around the same time as the 37th Division, and as it moved to into the Santa Ana District, it encountered little resistance and quickly set up patrols to secure the area. Thus, by February 10th, the XIV Corps had secured two sectors across the Pasig River, and along with the 11th Airborne to the south, they now had the ability to deploy their forces to encircle the city and cut off withdrawal routes for the Japanese soldiers stationed there. The 5th Cavalry moved from the west, taking the strategic area of Nielson Field, while the 8th Cavalry, and later the 12th Cavalry (which relieved the 8th Cavalry), made its way to Manila Bay. Furthermore, the 37th Division made contact with the 11th Airborne coming up from the south, completing the encirclement of Japanese forces in Manila.

The Japanese commander tasked with defending Manila, Admiral Sanji Iwabuchi, had originally planned to defend the city until the end, but as American forces began moving toward the city, Iwabuchi decided that the situation was so dire that he began planning for a withdrawal. First, he moved his headquarters to Fort McKinley, a few miles outside of the city, and then began planning a more general retreat.

As this was occurring, General Yokoyama of the Shimbu Group was planning for a counterattack against American forces near Manila. Yokoyama believed there was only one regiment of American troops near Manila and believed he had an opportunity to cut them off from the main attack force on Luzon. With Iwabuchi away from the city, Yokoyama halted the Manila Naval Defense Force from retreating out of Manila and had them hold their position in Manila pending the outcome of the Shimbu Group's counterattack.

The counterattack would consist of two columns. The northern column would attack across the Markina River, aiming for Novaliches Dam and Route 3 north of the city, while the southern column would also move across the Markina, then through the Balara Water Filters, before establishing contact with the northern wing at Grace Park. The 112th Cavalry, which had replaced the 12th Cavalry, faced the brunt of the northern column's counterattack between February 15th and 18th. After a series of skirmishes in which 300 Japanese soldiers were killed, the counterattack fell apart and the northern column retreated, and the southern column was caught as it was crossing the Marikina River when American artillery units attacked it on February 16th. For the next three days, the 7th and 8th Cavalry fought off their attempts to break through American lines, and when the southern column finally withdrew on the 19th, American troops had killed roughly 650 enemy soldiers. With the failure of the counterattacks, there was no hope of Japanese forces opening a gap in the American circle, and from that point on, the Shimbu Group had no further contact with the Manila Naval Defense Force, which was left on its own to attempt to repel American forces at Manila.

After stopping the Shimbu Group's counterattack, American forces turned their attention back to taking Manila. As the XIV Corps pushed in from the north and west, the 11th Airborne held their lines around Manila and also cut off the Abe Battalion of the Southern Luzon Force at Mabato Point. Between February 18th and 23rd, three infantry battalions, with support from artillery and tanks, attacked the Abe Battalion, killing 750 men while suffering only 60 casualties.

Within Manila, engagements between American and Japanese troops took the form of street fighting, with American troops being forced to slowly push forward and clear buildings and streets one at a time. As this was occurring, American artillery units and bombers took out most of the remaining Japanese mortars and artillery, reducing them to using light weapons, grenades and machine guns against the oncoming Americans.

Filipino citizens running from the fighting in Manila in February 1945

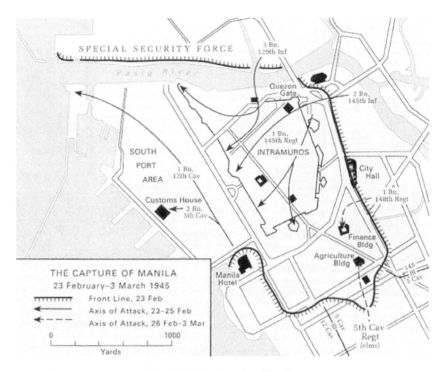

The Allied push against Manila

American troops pushed Japanese forces back block by block, finally leading up to the last stand by Japanese forces at the cluster of governmental buildings known as the Walled City. The Americans resorted to artillery bombardments for several days because American commanders believed Japanese troops had constructed a series of tunnels and bunkers in the Walled City that would be difficult for American infantry to assault without heavy bombardments before the final attack. On February 23rd, the ground assault began with the infantry advancing into the Walled City while being supported by tanks, artillery and mortars. Much of the subsequent fighting occurred between American infantry units and isolated pockets of Japanese troops who had sought cover from the artillery fire.

It took a little more than a day to finish clearing Japanese troops from the Walled City, and by late on the 24th, they had finished operations at the Walled City and nearby Fort Santiago. In total, the battle of Manila cost the XIV Corps 1,000 men killed and 5,500 wounded. The Japanese lost 16,000 men killed in the area around Manila, and the Manila Defense Force itself lost 12,500 men killed, with the rest being members of the Shimbu Group who had engaged

American troops either during the failed counterattack or in skirmishes around periphery of Manila.

In addition to the military casualties, large portions of the city were destroyed by the fighting, and the damage done to Filipino civilians was extensive. The Japanese had fought to the death across Manila, and Admiral Iwabuchi and his men had also presided over the systematic murder and rape of Filipino civilians. MacArthur had refused outright to countenance tactical airstrikes in support of his own troops for fear of killing civilians, which slowed the advance and increased American casualties. While this presented a classic moral-military conundrum, nobody can deny the moral integrity of MacArthur's command, but when the city fell at the end of February, an estimated 100,000 civilians were dead.

American troops in the Walled City on February 27, 1945

An aerial view of the devastated ruins of Manila in May 1945

Chapter 7: Mopping Up

As Manila was falling, Japanese commanders on Luzon had a decision to make regarding how to proceed with their defense of that island. Their main remaining goal was to deny the Americans the use of Manila Bay, a port that could be used as a staging area for an assault on the Japanese home islands. They could either deny the use of the bay by holding out at the Bataan peninsula, as the Americans had done in 1941-1942, or they could position themselves in northern Luzon and attempt to hold out there.

After securing Manila, the Sixth Army began moving to engage and destroy the Shobu and Shimbu Groups, the two largest Japanese troop concentrations remaining on Luzon. While the XIV Corps was fighting in Manila, the I Corps had positioned itself along the northern portion of the Central Plains, and after its victory against the Manila Defense Force, both portions of the Sixth Army were now ready for the next part of the operation. However, after the victory at Manila, MacArthur shifted tactics in a way that hampered the Sixth Army's ability to quickly engage and defeat the remaining Japanese soldiers on Luzon. With Japanese defeat at Luzon seemingly assured, MacArthur ordered a garrison force to be established in Manila and also siphoned off troops from Luzon to help retake central and southern Philippine islands that had been bypassed in the initial invasion of the nation.

Given the reduction in troop strength, the attacks against the Shimbu and Shobu Groups would be more difficult than had been originally anticipated. The Shimbu Group consisted of roughly

30,000 soldiers, and they were deployed along a defensive line that was aided by rugged, mountainous terrain. American operations against the Shimbu Group commenced on February 20th, when the 7th Cavalry marched through the Marikina Valley that led up to the Shimbu Group's positions. Behind the 7th Cavalry was the 8th Cavalry, which secured the town of Tagig and then also made its way through the Marikina Valley.

On February 23rd, the 7th Cavalry made contact with the forward elements of the Shimbu Group's defensive line and came under attack near Antipolo. The 7th and 8th Cavalry faced heavy fighting for the next week, during which they were barely able to gain any ground. The fighting was made more difficult by the fact that Japanese soldiers based their defense around a series of caves that were difficult for artillery to hit, forcing American troops to engage each cave and bunker and either kill or drive out the Japanese soldiers stationed within them.

The 6th Division also began marching toward the Shimbu Group's positions on February 22nd. They headed toward the northern section of the Japanese defenses, where they attacked positions located at Mount Pacawagan and Mount Mataba. Under fierce fighting, they were unable to dislodge Japanese soldiers from these locations, and by March 4th, American commanders decided to revise their plans. In their new plans, American forces would concentrate their efforts against the Shimbu Group's left, where they hoped to outflank Japanese positions. If this was successful, American troops could then get around Japanese defenses and attack their most fortified positions from behind.

On March 8th, the 1st Cavalry and 6th Infantry began their attack, while to the south, the 20th Infantry and 1st Infantry cleared what were believed to be the Shimbu Group's main supply route. The 1st Infantry was able to force its way a mile and a half forward, and by March 11, they had created a gap in the Japanese defenses. The 20th Infantry then moved in behind the 1st Infantry before heading to the east to attack a second section of the defense.

The Shimbu Group's commanding officer, General Yokoyama, became concerned about the penetration into his defenses and ordered that section of the perimeter to fall back to its secondary defense lines. He then ordered a counterattack on March 12th that involved a three-pronged assault by seven infantry battalions. Even in the beginning, this counterattack seemed destined to fail as American artillery quickly knocked out communication and command post positions that were crucial to coordinating the elements of the attack. The counterattack then devolved into isolated endeavors by Japanese units, and Yokoyama called it off on March 15th after having suffered losses amounting to two battalions of soldiers.

In the aftermath of the counterattack, American troops put renewed pressure on Japanese defenses. While their progress continued to be slow, American units advanced at four points along the defense perimeter, and they also drove a deep wedge along the Japanese left. American forces were unable to make further gains in the next few days, but General Yokoyama, believing that his situation was precarious, decided to pull his units on the left back across the Bosoboso

River. However, due to communication problems along the line, these units did not begin their retreat until March 22nd, and on that day, an attack by American 6th and 43rd Division units coincided with the retreat. The Americans therefore encountered little resistance as they pushed forward and gained important positions at Mounts Baytangan, Yabang, and Caymayuman.

With the withdrawal and loss on their left, Japanese forces in that area were able, in the short-term, to remain in the field, but they now faced the possibility of being flanked and encircled, thus destabilizing the entire Japanese defense perimeter. As this was occurring, a renewed push against the center of the Japanese line in late March further weakened their position. Although fighting would be slow as American troops advanced, the defense had been compromised, and after taking Ipo Dam, the center of the Japanese line had collapsed. Thanks to the strength of the Japanese defense along hill and mountain positions, coupled with their use of caves, trenches and tunnels, continued fighting would occur through late May, but the Shimbu Group had lost cohesiveness, and their ability to mount a serious threat to American troops had been negated. From this point forward, American units engaged in mopping up operations that involved slowly moving forward and killing or driving out isolated groups of Japanese soldiers who remained in the field.

The Shobu Group was the second major Japanese force remaining in the field in Luzon, and unlike the Shimbu Group, they had planned to withdraw into northern Luzon, where they would attempt to hold out for as long as possible against American forces. The Shobu Group deployed its units to create a triangle, with its points at Baguio, Bontoc, and Bambang, and with a fourth sector in the Cagayan Valley which supplied Japanese forces. The 32nd Division was ordered to attack the Shobu Group, and they began moving out in early February where they reached the town of Santa Maria and then continued further on toward the entrances of the Arboredo and Agno River Valleys. For the next week, the 32nd Division engaged Japanese a series of outpost defenses before finally coming across the main Japanese defensive line in the area on the Villa Verde Trail.

Like the 32nd Division, the 25th Division also began operations in northern Luzon in early February. During reconnaissance operations, the 25th Division found that Japanese troops had concentrated in their area, meaning that they had positioned troops to defend the approaches to their defensive triangle from this direction as well. Aerial reconnaissance during this period also discovered the Baguio-Aritao supply road, which connected Japanese troops at Bagui and Bambang. American commanders realized that if they could take the supply road, they would be able to isolate Japanese troops at the two locations, so they decided to target the supply road in their attacks against the Shobu Group.

Aside from the two American divisions, Filipino guerrilla units (known as the USAFIP) also operated in tandem with the Americans in northern Luzon. Guerrilla units were tasked with reconnaissance operations and attacking Japanese patrols. Over time, their operations expanded to the point that Filipino guerrillas comprised roughly one division of combat troops against the Shobu Group.

American commanders chose to begin their efforts in northern Luzon against Bambang. The 25th and 32nd Divisions would be involved in these efforts, while the 44th Division would occupy Japanese forces at Baguio to keep them from reinforcing Bambang.

During late February and early March, the 33rd Division probed Japanese defenses. On the east side, 33rd Division troops were able to take Japanese positions in a ridged area that was referred to as the Hill 600-1500 line. Elsewhere, American troops had problems gaining traction against entrenched defenses, such as along Route 11, where the 71st Infantry was only able to get within a mile and a half of its stated objective of an area called Camp 2.

Meanwhile, the 33rd Division commander, Major General Percy Clarkson, was upset that his forces were only being used to hold Japanese forces in place at Baguio during this initial phase of the mission. When he realized that Japanese forces were engaging in a withdrawal all along its line, he argued that he should be allowed to push his troops forward to take a more forward position. 33rd Division reconnaissance units moved forward beginning on March 7th, and they were surprised to find almost no resistance along the western portion of the Japanese defenses, which allowed them to take Aringay and Caba. Other units pushed Japanese troops back from the hills at the entrance to the Tuba Trail. The seeming lack of defenses in this area convinced Clarkson to focus on this area, and by mid-March, he had made plans to utilize both regular troops and guerrilla units to make a push on Baguio. American forces first took the port town of San Fernando against a 3,000 man defense force, and this cleared the way along Route 9 for the drive on Baguio.

Aside from losing territory leading up to Baguio, Japanese forces had the added problems of supply difficulties, with American air strikes on supply roads restricting the supplies that made it to Japanese troops. Before the end of March, front-line troops were receiving less than a quarter of their daily rations, and starvation and diet-related diseases were taking its toll on Japanese troop-strength. Yamashita, realizing the precarious position that his forces at Baguio were in, ordered Japanese civilians and governmental officials to evacuate the city. For his soldiers, however, he ordered them to remain to defend the city for as long as possible.

In early April, American forces made their push for Baguio. The 129th Infantry broke through at Sablan in a battle involving artillery and medium tanks. The 148th Infantry then secured Route 9 through the town of Calot, and other American units secured supply depots along the area that Japanese troops were retreating from. Finally, between April 11th and 15th, American artillery, airplanes, and tank units targeted and destroyed nearly all artillery pieces that Japanese forces in the area had at their disposal. In order to try to shore up his position, General Sato, commander of Japanese troops at Baguio, sent two infantry companies to a barrio two miles southeast of Calot, but before they arrived, American troops had passed that point and had taken the town of

Yagyagan. This episode highlighted the dysfunction that Japanese commanders were experiencing by this point.

Beyond Yagyagan, Japanese forces had created a defensive position at the Irisan gorge, an area with defensible high ground positions that were well positioned to fire down into Route 9, which passed through the gorge. Elements of the 148th Infantry began the assault by engaging in a frontal attack on the Japanese positions, while other units made an enveloping maneuver from the sides. After heavy fighting, the 148th was able to secure the area. American units continued to push forward, where they overcame a series of hill positions leading into Baguio, and by April 22nd, they were ready to make their final push into the town.

On April 22nd, two battalions from the 130th Infantry moved in from the west, while a battalion from the 75th Infantry came in from the south. These units met heavy resistance from Japanese troops, but elsewhere the 123rd Infantry was able to make important gains that triggered a withdrawal by some sections of the defense. The speed of the American advance forced a general Japanese withdrawal at this location as well, and by April 24th, the 33rd Division held most of Baguio. While losing this important location was a blow to the Japanese, they were able to get 10,000 troops out ahead of the American advance, which they could subsequently use to reinforce other sections of the their defensive perimeter.

The 25th and 32nd Divisions on the Bambang front they quickly made contact with Japanese troops and then began assessing plans for an assault on Bambang. In late February, the 126th Infantry of the 32nd Division attacked two Japanese delaying positions, while American patrols in the nearby Agno Valley found no sign of Japanese troops. To the west. in the Arboredo Valley, American units found the opposite: Japanese forces had set up strong outposts here to stop an advance. Units attacking from three directions compressed the defense line, and after heavy fighting accompanied by artillery support, elements of the 127th Infantry were able to break through the outpost line on February 24th. As Japanese troops from the 10th Reconnaissance division (which had been manning the outpost) retreated, they were pursued by the 127th, which continued forcing contact with the retreating troops and harassing them. Finally, as the 10th Reconnaissance withdrew to the Salacsac Pass area, they were reinforced by two companies of infantry and one under-strength artillery battalion. As the Japanese units were being reinforced, the 127th Infantry was joined by the 2nd Tank Battalion to increase their troop-strength in that vicinity.

Since Salacsac Pass was a strong defensive position, it seemed as though the opposing forces were headed toward a stalemate, and much of the month of March involved American attempts to dislodge Japanese troops from their high-ground positions, while Japanese troops made use of their terrain advantage to repulse American attacks. The 10th Reconnaissance and their reinforcements also were able to fall back to secondary and tertiary defense positions at Salacsac Pass, giving them an increased ability to delay and harass the American advance. In fact, the

128th Infantry and 2nd Tank Battalion had not yet broken through by April 5th, and between the 5th and 17th, American soldiers at Salacsac Pass were suffering large numbers of casualties.

After more reinforcements, American troops spent the month of April attacking a series of Japanese hill positions. Japanese soldiers delayed the push as long as possible, and in late April they sent a counterattack that failed to allow them to gain territory against the Americans. American forces finally began to make headway in early May as they engaged in an enveloping movement involving battalions from the 127th and 128th Infantry as the 126th Infantry engaged troops in adjacent areas. The attack was successful and occurred so quickly that American forces reached the Villa Verde Trail.

It was at this point that the 32nd Division was close to linking up with the 25th Division near Santa Fe. With that, the last obstacle for American forces before Bambang was Balete Pass, which the 27th Infantry began attacking on April 27th. Aiding the 27th Infantry was the 35th Infantry, and these two units fought their way up Kapintalan Ridge while the 161st Infantry came in from the west to begin an enveloping movement against Japanese positions. This movement surprised the Japanese troops, and by May 4th, the Americans had captured Balete Pass and had moved beyond it. Helping the troops engaged on the Bambang Front was that at this point, Baguio had been secured, and reinforcements could now help bolster the American troop-strength.

The last major action along the Bambang Front occurred at Santa Fe. From May 14-22, the 27th Infantry cleared enemy troops around Kanami Ridge while the 161th Infantry took a strong enemy position at Mount Haruna. Continued fighting occurred along the Bambang Front, but this mainly took the form of invading pockets of Japanese forces. By May 29th, American units were in the process of surrounding Japanese troops at Bambang when Yamashita sent orders for a withdrawal from that location. The fighting had been extremely costly for both sides, as the 2nd Tank Division and 10th Division suffered casualties amounting to 13,500 men, while roughly two-thirds of the 20,750 soldiers at the Bambang Front were killed. (Smith, p.538)

The withdrawal at Bambang, coupled with the losses at Baguio, forced General Yamashita to order a general withdrawal of the Shobu Group to their last-stand positions, known to American commanders as the Kiangan Pocket, on June 15th. At the Kiangan Pocket, the American 6th Division moved up Route 4 before quickly breaking through a portion of the perimeter that was being manned by the Japanese 105th Division. As this was occurring, UFAIP guerrillas attacked from the direction of the Cagayan Valley. The situation for Japanese troops was one of extreme disorganization. Some troops were still trying to make their way to the last-stand position, while others were trapped by American forces.

General Krueger took advantage of the confusion among Japanese units by pressing his advantage, looking to move his forces quickly forward with the 37th Division moving up Route 5 through Santa Fe and Bagabag while the 6th Division would move in a more northerly direction through Route 4. This movement would surround and restrict the retreating Japanese troops. Between June 1st and 4th, Japanese antitank units tried to slow the American pursuit, but although they engaged the 776th Tank Battalion which was reinforcing the 129th Infantry, they were unable to do enough damage to delay their progress. Within the next few days American troops secured the towns of Aritao, Bayombong, and Bagabag.

The American advance continued through mid-June, where they reached the Cagayan Valley. Fighting within the valley occurred when the American 37th Division engaged with Japanese soldiers from the Yuguchi Detachment, who were retreating up Route 5. The 37th Division killed 600 Japanese soldiers and captured another 285 (Smith, p.569). By this time, Krueger believed that Japanese forces were on the verge of defeat, so he sent additional troops in the form of the 11th Infantry of the USAFIP.

By the end of June, Japanese troops, who had been harried and harassed for the majority of their retreat, had reached their final positions. American units had penetrated into northern Luzon to the point that there were two separate elements of the Shobu Group. One, comprised of 13,000 soldiers, was located at Sierra Madre. Meanwhile, the main body of 52,000 troops was positioned at the Japanese last-stand area. Although in raw numbers it seemed that Japanese troops still had the ability to threaten American forces, most of these soldiers were ill-equipped and were suffering from starvation and disease. As it turned out, a final confrontation in northern Luzon never occurred. Instead, American troops focused on containing Japanese forces, and the remaining Shobu Group units actually stayed in the field until the end of the war, at which point they finally surrendered. Mopping up operations also occurred on islands in the central and southern Philippines, but with the capture of Luzon, American forces were now prepared to begin building the military infrastructure for bombing missions and a possible invasion of the Japanese home islands.

Bibliography

Breuer, William B. (1986). Retaking The Philippines: America's Return to Corregidor & Bataan, 1944–1945. St Martin's Press. ASIN B000IN7D3Q.

Dower, John. *War Without Mercy: Pacific War*. New York: Random House, 1986.

Leary, William M. (2004). We Shall Return!: MacArthur's Commanders and the Defeat of Japan, 1942–1945. University Press of Kentucky. ISBN 0-8131-9105-X.

Mellnik, Stephen Michael (1981). Philippine War Diary, 1939–1945. Van Nostrand Reinhold. ISBN 0-442-21258-5.

Morison, Samuel Eliot (1958). Leyte: June 1944 – Jan 1945, vol. 12 of History of United States Naval Operations in World War II. Little, Brown and Company. ISBN 0-316-58317-0.

Morison, Samuel Eliot (2001). The Liberation of the Philippines: Luzon, Mindanao, the Visayas 1944–1945, vol. 13 of History of United States Naval Operations in World War II (Reissue ed.). Castle Books. ISBN 0-7858-1314-4.

Norling, Bernard (2005). The Intrepid Guerrillas Of North Luzon. University Press of Kentucky. ISBN 0-8131-9134-3.

Smith, Robert Ross. *Triumph in the Philippines: The War in the Pacific*. Washington, DC: Center of Military History, 1993.

Spector, Ronald. *Eagle Against the Sun: The American War With Japan*. New York: Free Press, 2012.

Made in United States
North Haven, CT
04 April 2025

67594745R00065